I MARRIED A COWBOY

By

CONSTANCE DOUGLAS REEVES

EAKIN PRESS Fort Worth, Texas
www.EakinPress.com

This book is dedicated to Waldemar, its horses,
and the little girls who ride them.

Library of Congress Cataloging-in-Publication Data:

Reeves, Constance Douglas, 1901–
  I married a cowboy / by Constance Douglas Reeves. — 1st ed.
    p.   cm.
  ISBN 1-57168-051-9
  1. Reeves, Constance Douglas, 1901–   . 2. Reeves, Jack, d. 1985. 3. Cowboys —
Texas — Kimble County — Biography. 4. Ranchers — Texas — Kimble County —
Biography. 5. Ranch life — Texas — Kimble County. 6. Kimble County (Tex.) —
Biography. I. Title.
F391.4.R44A3 1996
976.4'878063'092–dc20
[B]   95-36442
                                                                              CIP

Preface

What is Waldemar? To the Native Americans it meant "Sea of Woods" but to others it is a place to go to spend the summer; a place to learn and play; a place to form lasting friendships and gather fond memories.

From the very instant one passes between the impressive wrought iron gates fortified by a wall of finely chiseled native stone, the spell is cast.

It isn't just the beauty of the waterfront; although it is incredibly beautiful. Here the crystal-clear waters of the Guadalupe River mirror the stately centuries-old cypress trees standing like sentinels on both banks.

It isn't just the canopy of steel blue sky and gently floating clouds still lightly flushed from the kiss of the rising sun. Nighttime generously sprinkles this same sky with myriads of dancing stars just inches beyond the reach of one's hand.

It isn't just the brightness of the harvest moon, which causes the bullfrogs to croak, the whippoorwills to cry, and the wind to whisper softly through the trees.

It isn't just the chain of lacy cedar trees framing the rough and rugged hills, which climb higher and higher in the distance.

It isn't just the smiles of snaggle-toothed, freckle-faced little girls giggling with childish delight.

Yes, it is! It is a composite of all of this, and a lot more, that makes Waldemar so special.

Little did I know that day in June 1936 when I arrived on the campus that my life would change so drastically. It was there that I met the cowboy, who later became my husband. It was there that I learned the true value of loyalty, friendship, and sportsmanship. It was there that I collected fifty-eight years of priceless memories.

My job was to teach little girls to enjoy the art of horsemanship — to ride safely and correctly, to establish a relationship with their four legged mounts which would remain with them forever.

Most of the camp horses were supplied by the director's uncle, who was a rodeo producer. Col. W. T. Johnson prided himself on having a high-class, world-renowned show and chose his horses accordingly.

Once, while the rodeo was showing at Madison Square Gardens in New York, the colonel took Billy Sunday, a black and white paint gelding, to the top of the Empire State Building as one of his advertising schemes. Needless to say that hailed as the only horse to have ever accomplished this feat — each of the little girls clamored to ride him. Even today, where we are in our fourth generation of campers, I hear: "My grandmother said she rode a horse named Billy Sunday. Do you remember him?"

Memories! Memories! So many names, faces, experiences flashing through my mind — so many faithful horses, so many good friends, so much to be thankful for.

There are memories of adventuresome and outgoing girls with confidence and courage, who exhibited great talent and skill. Many of these former campers of all ages are still involved with showing, breeding programs, or just riding for pleasure.

Then there are memories of the timid, even less talented girls, who struggled, achieved, and enjoyed their triumph over fear and inexperience.

There are memories of good, big-hearted and kind horses who wore their hearts out in long years of faithful service. Memories of Teddy, Monarch, Gold Mine, Pal, Red Apple, Partner, Mr. Blue.

I am reminded of a very special horse's dedication to his work. Moon Glow was a handsome fifteen hands bay gelding with a free going style and gentle disposition. He was probably twenty or over, at the time, but our horses seldom have a problem with age. We like to buy them after they have settled, six or seven years old, and keep them until they can no longer safely carry a child on their backs.

Moon Glow had always been a favorite with both students and instructors due to his dependability but he was getting slow — especially in the rocks. One day I happened to be ahead of him as we came down the hill from the Ladies' Leg Tree, and I watched the peculiar manner in which he was stepping. He would lift one foot, fan it around before shifting weight as though he was feeling his way. As soon as the classes had left the corral, I walked over to the rail where he was standing and looked Moon Glow directly in the face. There was no responding reaction for the poor animal was totally blind. How long this condition had existed I had no idea, but it could have been several years since his behavior was perfectly normal. Big John and Dusty, his buddies, were always on hand to lead him from the corral, to pasture, between trees, and to the hay rack. I made it a practice to watch how one, or both, of the buddies would wait at the gate until they had him following safely behind. Some years later we had a similar instance when Smokey went blind, and his buddy Gene became the "seeing eye companion."

Horses have a tendency to run in pairs, or even groups of threes, fours, or fives. My heart has bled many times when something bad has happened to a member of one of these groups and the survivor shows his grief by nickering throughout the day and night or even refusing to eat or drink for several days.

Our highly paid meteorologists might predict weather more accurately if they could watch the conduct of horses. When a horse, at liberty, kicks up his heels, tucks his head, and starts to run — look out — the weather is going to change. Rain, a windshift, — something very different is brewing in the air.

Yes, Waldemar horses are very special, but the girls who ride or rode them have made it all worthwhile.

I recall the struggle I had my first year at the camp to get anyone to take English riding. Most of the girls, that first term, were from the West Texas ranching area, Del Rio, Plano, Amarillo, Fort Worth, Wichita Falls, or Midland and their fathers were horrified at the idea of their daughters bouncing up and down on "postage stamps."

My will prevailed; the girls took to the hornless saddles like fish to water and their parents were treated to one of the most spectacular of Quadrilles at the end camp. Today, we still have children or relatives following in their paths.

Campers from Oklahoma City, Houston, Port Arthur, Austin, Little Rock, or Shreveport have always excelled in English riding, and it has been a challenge to the instructors to devise means of maintaining their interest. Jumping, Monkey Drill (Acrobatics) as well as Quadrille attract most of these talented, and today they are learning to play Polo-crosse.

High on the shelf of fond memories is that of a little girl from Breckenridge who cried on every ride her first year at camp but stood up on her mount while cantering across the Athletic Field at her Horse Show her final year.

To be greeted by radiant and sunny faces; to see improvement in performance; to hear squeals of delight at a special achievement; to be assaulted by pleas to ride a favorite horse; to observe little faces lifted to plant a kiss on a fuzzy nose; to see tiny arms gently caressing an outstretched neck have made all the many long hours in the saddle so worthwhile. There are no regrets, only memories — fond, rewarding, everlasting. A final salute to Waldemar for making it all so dear to me.

CHAPTER 1

He had heard the roar of the crowd in the packed arena for the last time. Never again would he back his horse into the chute, pull down his hat, and nod for the calf. There would be no more blast of trumpets, blaze of lights, stomping of feet as the announcer shouts: "That's it, folks! That's the time to beat!"

The cowboy made his last professional rodeo appearance in 1940. The trophy belt buckles, silver-trimmed hatbands, and monogrammed chaps were replaced by flat heel boots, faded jeans, and sweat-stained Stetsons. The cowboy became a stockman with a ranch to manage and a wife to help him.

The man I married is more than a ridin', ropin', pistol packin' cowpoke staggering through the doors of a saloon or dashing to the rescue of a fair damsel in distress. He belongs to a new brand of men which is a combination cowboy-rancher-stockman. The life of this new man still has the color and romance depicted on the silver screen, and his days are filled with danger and action. But there also is stability and promise of a tomorrow.

When, at the break of day, my husband reaches for his saddle there is anticipation in the rising sun. Then later there is satisfaction when he removes that saddle as the setting sun sinks from view in all its fiery glory.

Ranching calls upon the strength and stamina of these men of the range for they must spend endless hours in the saddle alternately being roasted or refrigerated. They suffer cuts and bruises, parched lips, barbed wire pricks, festered sores from

1

mesquite or cactus thorns, dust-red eyes, chapped hands, and frostbitten ears, but they also have their comforts and exhilarating moments.

Most of the stockman's days and many of his nighttime hours are devoted to the demands of the animals dependent upon him. He must be capable of administering to those demands even as a doctor assumes the care of his human patients. A horse with colic, a heifer trying to have her first calf, unprotected fresh shorn goats, and an approaching storm are a few of the many problems which plague the cowboy's off-duty hours.

There are no teachers in the ranchman's world. Ingenuity, common sense, and experience are the equation which solves most problems. The answer is correct if it attains the desired result with the least amount of effort.

This modern day cowboy must possess many talents for his responsibilities are as numerous as a leopard's spots. Whether selecting and purchasing a registered bull or mending a broken fence the act is only one of the many activities which confront him. He must be a scientist with a knowledge of minerals and vitamins, agriculturist familiar with soil control methods, animal psychologist able to diagnose the problem.

The diversity of talents required to operate a ranch successfully is unbelievable. The boss must be veterinarian, mechanic, plumber, welder, carpenter, blacksmith, diplomat, overseer, and common laborer. The knowledge my husband acquired, which enables him to perform these many tasks, is the result of trial and error and of many long hours beginning where he left off yesterday. It seems like he never gets through.

Neither does his wife. She has, in addition to her household chores, almost as many jobs as does her husband. Where he is doctor, she is nurse; he mechanic, she hands him the tools; he fencebuilder, she holds the wirestretcher while he drives in the staples. She opens and shuts gates, runs errands, fills syringes, counts stock out of the chute, starts the spraying machine, and acts as bookkeeper. She sympathizes, encourages, suggests (with timidity), and turns a deaf ear to those volcanic grumblings and mumblings when things go wrong.

Jack, my cowboy husband, stands tall as the spreading chestnut tree with arms outspread to the needs of the ranch. I am the ever present shadow.

My heart never ceases to jump with joy when, at the end of day, I see a lone horse and rider trotting down the dusty trail. It is that time of day the country woman likes best. That bewitching hour of candlelight when the whip-o'-will calls to its mate, the locust and crickets chirp, and the loo of the milk cow can be heard above the whine of the windmill.

Stockmen take pleasure in knowing the needs of the animals dependent upon them and in being able to administer to those needs. They also take pleasure in being indispensable in service to mankind by raising healthier beef and mutton for America's tables and a better quality of wool and mohair for her clothing. Added to the satisfaction of a worthwhile life of service and accomplishment is the realization that no two days will be alike.

There is nothing as thrill-packed and exciting as life on the open range. Each hour is crammed with sixty minutes of uncharted activity. Here, in the great out of doors, even the inertia of an inactive day is challenged by the unpredictable.

If it isn't the weather which makes the difference, there is always the possibility that we will find another sheriff handcuffed to a tree, a plane will crash in the pasture, a wounded deer will attack a neighbor, or a child will be bitten by a rattlesnake.

These are just a few of the unpredictable events with which we have had to cope.

CHAPTER 2

It seems only yesterday that an automobile, with a woman and her husband riding in it, sped down the highway. There was nothing about the general appearance of the man with his clear eyes intent on the road ahead and his weather worn hands gripping the steering wheel to indicate anything unusual. He could just as easily have been a rancher returning from an auction with livestock in a trailer as a man coming from his wedding with his bride on the seat beside him.

Quiet, sedate yet blissfully aware of the other's presence, they rode in that deep comfortable silence of thoughtful meditation while their car rolled smoothly along. Excited and elated as I, that woman, was over the prospect of getting to the ranch, the magic of the nuptial ceremony still engulfed me in a misty enchantment.

Suddenly the lingering memory was drowned by the splatter of flying gravel. With a slight jolt the car slowed, turned, and came to an abrupt stop. My husband's voice was steady as he said, "You can get out and open the gate."

My eyes widened in surprise as, with puzzled astonishment, I turned and looked at his face. There, playing across the corners of his mouth, was the beginning of a big smile as he assured me saying, "That, my dear, is the cowboy's way of carrying his bride across the threshold of her new home."

I smiled back at him, stepped out, and lifted the horseshoe latch on the gate. The car passed through but I stood there with the latch in my hand. For a long time I stood still and thought, *This is the beginning of our married life. This is our homecoming. With the simple act of opening a gate our partnership has been consummated. Before us lies the future with its promise of understanding and comradeship.*

I stepped back into the automobile knowing that a seed of togetherness had been planted with that act. Together the cowboy and his wife would face the future side by side.

It was slow driving on the narrow and winding road with darkness gathering all around us. A sharp turn revealed the house standing in a blaze of lights, which were reflected on the vehicles parked along the fence.

"What are all those lights?" I asked Jack.

"Must be a welcome home party," was his answer. "It's the largest bunch I've ever seen. Someone has surely been spreading the news."

When he finished speaking, I turned around and reached for my hat on the back seat but he put out a restraining hand. "Please don't put it on. Your hair is beautiful and besides," he hesitated, "you'll look more like one of them. Not so fancy and citified."

Then I watched his hand go to his tie, loosen it, and unfasten the top button of his shirt. As if by accident, the fingers slipped through the well groomed hair and left it tousled in their wake.

This time, as the car came to a sliding stop, I was lifted high and carried into the house storybook style. I looked down on a sea of new but friendly faces and was touched by their obvious sincerity. I saw that the gathering was an assortment of men, women, and children, and I rejoiced in their informality. It was enough for them that I was "Jack's wife" for, I soon learned, he was a great favorite with the neighbors.

When the initial excitement of seeing and greeting died down, the men drifted toward the corrals, the children went out into the yard, and the women began to arrange the food they had provided. They uncovered cakes and pies, fried chicken, and all the other good things to eat. Skilled and loving hands had been busy making these flavorful dishes, each a worthy contender for highest honors at a county fair. Added to the fragrant aroma of well cooked food was the tantalizing odor of boiling coffee.

The call: "Come and get it" was answered by much laughter

and friendly banter and the scraping of well filled plates. When all had eaten, the men and children retired to the front porch and the women to the kitchen to tidy up before joining their families.

The low musical hum of soft voices, a flipped cigarette's arched glow in the deep darkness, and the gentle tap-tap of the porch swing blended with the whispering of the wind through the trees. Shrouded in the black draperies of night the bodies of the men and women became spectral forms outlined against the lamp light's glow from within. Soon old Mrs. Foster judiciously proclaimed, "Lands alive! It's getting late and we have a long way to go."

Congratulations and good-byes were hastily completed as the families collected children and scattered belongings and crawled into their vehicles. Cries of: "You all come" drifted back and echoed through the hills. The taillights of the last car glowed red against the distant sky as it climbed the ridge and disappeared. Standing there, watching the glow grow dim, listening to the echoes of the mingled calls and pleasant night noises, the man and woman smiled at each other and, arm in arm, entered the house.

CHAPTER 3

Ranching imposes an endless chain of events upon the stockman. He sees the months merge into years and the years roll by as the cycle repeats itself.

September starts the wheel revolving with the shearing of the goats, after which comes work with the sheep and cattle. Fences must be kept in repair, windmills running, water troughs cleaned, and a continuous check must be made on all livestock for injuries, sickness, or loss of flesh.

There is the unpredictable blending of marking, drenching, shearing, tagging, roofing, spraying, and vaccinating. There is a perpetual shifting and moving of animals from one pasture to another, of putting in the males during mating season and taking them out, separating the young, culling, and marketing. There is the inevitable amount of riding, rounding up, and driving. The dull continuity of feeding.

Jack explained all this to me that first morning at the ranch. I began to see him as a man on an adventure like those early pioneers who crossed virgin land seeking new horizons. There were no maps, no signs, no roads, just a strong will to succeed and a lot of faith as Jack has.

That first morning he took me on a ride to the top of one of the highest hills. The climb didn't seem long nor steep but it provided us with a view for miles in all directions. We could see the stock grazing in the open, the ranch house, windmills and tanks, pens and fields. Way off in the distance there were cars on the road leading to town, and we could even see the neighbor's dividing fences.

From our bedroom window, earlier, I had looked toward those hills and watched the spectacle of the rising sun in all its unpaintable splendor. The low clouds which obscured the peak of the range and hovered over the valleys were delicately tinged with pink. Slowly, their color darkened to a rosy gold as the soft fluffy cumulus drifted higher and unveiled the rock ledges still glistening with dew. Steadily as if pulled by an invisible cord the clouds climbed and took on the rich warmth of the sun. A magic serape seemed to be spread over the countryside.

There was the sunshine of happiness in my heart as I turned from the window and walked into the kitchen.

We had just started to eat when a belated member of the welcoming party pecked lightly at our front door. The words of greeting, "Come in and have a —" froze on my husband's lips when, opening the door, there was no one there. I had about decided we were the recipients of a practical joke when the cowboy called to him.

"Look. Now your welcome is complete." Laughing, he pointed and said, "See what has come to pay its respects."

There beneath the roof's protruding eaves, high above the door, was a yellow head woodpecker peering at us with cocked head. Its beady black eyes glaring over the chisel-like beak seemed to be regarding us with suspicion. Amused at the unexpected visitor we returned to the table. By this time the sun was high in the sky and Jack saddled the horses while I washed the dishes.

A few hundred yards from the barn we came upon a spring fed creek which followed the shape of an "S" as it circled around the house and corrals. Its winding course necessitated crossing twice before beginning the climb up and out of the valley.

I drank in the natural beauty of the stream as we stopped to water the horses. Against a background of sheer white chalk cliffs, huge boulders lined the sides of the water and formed crevices from which sprang large clusters of swordfern. Sparkling drops from hidden springs dripped timidly, leaping with fright as they trickled and splashed into the running water beneath.

I didn't realize then, as we crossed a field and followed a winding trail up the hillside, how important that creek was to become in the future.

The panorama, from on high, held my attention but not Jack's. He was watching a swarming, circling bunch of buzzards just below us. These vultures never carry anything but bad news and serve as the stockman's messengers of distress. The sight of a number of them fluttering aloft and settling, signals something is dead or dying. They swoop down on the lifeless object, leaving a few perched on guard in nearby trees.

My husband read their aerial signal and knew he had to investigate. No time can be lost in locating and identifying their target.

He found a dead deer caught in the fence. The back legs of the deer, in jumping, had become hopelessly entwined in the wires. Today ranchers are building their new fences with the top two strands of wire further apart to prevent this happening.

I observed the expression on Jack's face as he came back to where I was waiting. It gave me an insight into that characteristic of the woodsman that I have never been able to understand. There is nothing which seems to upset him more than the sight of a dead animal and buzzards feeding on the carcass. Perhaps the explanation is that his work is dedicated to the preservation and protection of animals.

That first short ride about the place prepared me for the years to come. It gave me a glimpse of the grandeur, the splendor, as well as the pathos of life in the great out of doors. I saw that the stockman is an organization within himself who can acknowledge no planned rule of procedure. He is challenged to perform to the best of his ability on the spur of the minute whatever the demand may be.

CHAPTER 4

Deep in the center of Texas lies Kimble County, the very heart of the gigantic state's productive ranching region, known as the Hill Country. This range land, across which the icy winds of winter spread thin layers of snow, is magically turned to a sea of green by that sorceress, spring.

Junction, the county seat, almost obscured by large groves of giant pecan trees, rests in a valley surrounded by the two forks of the Llano River which merge nearby. It serves as the gateway to the cattle industry of the North, sheep and goat dynasty of the Central area, and the Winter Gardens to the South. It ranks as one of the oldest pioneer towns of Texas with a heritage of the Old West among its citizens.

We can see the glow from the city lights at our headquarters ranch on a clear night. Jack can also see, as he rests on our front porch at noon, a different picture. He sees the magnificent emerald turf in the valleys framed in its embossed tiffany setting of a chain of hills. There are fertile valleys and spring-fed creeks, fields and protective cover in his sight as he overlooks the rangeland.

Close at hand there are the barns, dipping vats, squeeze chute, and holding pens. He sees the windmill and watering troughs, the cypress tank, loading dock, and living quarters for the ranch hands.

Further away, he sees where fat cattle loll in the shade of

twisted and gnarled mesquite trees, sheep scrape for acorns, turkey clatter after cedar berries, and goats reach for tender leaves.

Our ranch house is just ten miles, as a crow flies, from Junction, where the streets come alive on Saturday afternoons when all of us from the country gather to do our week's shopping. The men squat on their heels, sit on the curbs, or lean across car hoods as they discuss the price of feed or need of rain. The women collect in the stores, crowding the aisles, eager to learn or pass on bits of gossip.

We will long remember what happened on one of those Saturday afternoons. Jack sat in the barber chair getting a hair cut when a man, clutching his stomach with bloody hands ran through screaming, "I've been shot! He got me."

He ran out the back door, stumbled, and died.

I, along with several other ladies, heard the shots from inside the grocery store. Those who had been on the street and witnessed the shooting gave us their version of what happened.

The two men, both known to be hotheaded, had argued over a game of pool. The first one pulled a gun, called the other a name, and threatened to shoot him. Angered and insulted, the second man accused the other of being a coward hiding behind a gun and dared him to wait until he, too, could get a gun.

The first man was standing in the middle of the street when the other returned. Apparently none of the observers took the situation seriously for no effort was made to stop the men.

It looked like the reenactment of an oldtime "shoot out" in a bad Western movie. Indeed, that was what it was, only this one was for real.

The men placed themselves, turned, and fired. Mr. Adams fell in his tracks but the other man ran across the street and through the barber shop before collapsing.

This, of course, was an isolated incident, but the Old West spirit still lingers in the hearts of many of the men in our area. The fathers and grandfathers of some of the men who worked part-time for us rode the cattle trails to Kansas and were part of the Old West. The experience of these men was helpful to Jack when working the varieties of stock over so many acres.

Checking the twenty sections of land is a full-time job for Jack, four or five laborers and the extra hands we hire when there is special work to be done. We like to keep a family or two living

11

on the place, but they don't stay very long. There has been a procession of them. Some stay a year or two; others move in and out so quickly I don't even remember their names.

I do, though, remember J. L. and his wife, Tince. I remember taking her to the doctor that afternoon. He told her to drink a cup of castor oil before retiring, and she'd be fine.

At midnight that night the sound we heard above the thunder and pounding rain was J. L. beating on our door. The telephone was out, Tince was in labor, and he wanted Jack to take him to get the doctor.

After the men had gone, I went over to stay with the young woman. Standing there beside the bed, holding her hand, I was overcome with the realization that I lacked the qualifications to cope with the situation. What if the doctor didn't get there in time? Should I raise the window and pray that the fairy tale Stork would find its way inside? Should I try to locate a piece of rope to tie on the infant's feet as I had often seen Jack do when assisting at the delivery of a calf?

Fortunately the doctor and baby arrived at the same time. The only thing I was asked to do was clean up the little girl, and even then, I didn't do a very good job. Removing the residue of castor oil with water isn't easy.

CHAPTER 5

It seems like shearing time is always just around the corner for the crew makes five trips to the ranch each year. For days before they arrive we are out in the pastures before daylight and seldom finish until after dark. After gathering, we have to run the stock through the cutting chute which enables the rancher to separate the goats and send them in opposite directions. There is not a doubt in my mind that I make a good hand when riding, but I'm a dismal failure at any other type of work.

Once, when we had to cut the goats, there wasn't anyone to help but Jack, Juan, a new man, and "guess who?"

When Juan and I tried to put the stubborn brutes through the chute, they would stop, turn around, crawl over or under each other, anything but go forward. We were getting nowhere fast when Jack called to me, "You come here and work the gate. I'll help Juan."

At my new position working the gate I stood at the front proudly watching the flow of upturned faces moving toward me.

"For C—'s sake, do something!" Jack shouted in exasperation. "You're supposed to separate the males from the females."

"What do you want me to do?" I fired back. "How do you expect me to tell Mr. from Mrs. goat, looking at them from the front end?"

Needless to say, I was sent back to work with Juan. Jack thought a dog might help. It did. The dog, with the help of Juan and me, got the job done.

Here on the elevated and fertile Edward's Plateau, where conditions are tight, raising of sheep and Angoras is a lucrative enterprise. Wool and mohair fleeces are in great demand; the prices are right. The nice thing is that the animals do not have to be sacrificed. The fleece of the young, kid and lamb, bring about twice as much on the market as does that of grown animals.

The shearers arrived on time. They looked like a band of roving gypsies as they drew up to the corrals. Santana, the patron, came first in his battered pickup with the shearing machine in tow. Several sets of eyes peered at us from beneath the tattered tarp billowing in the pickup's wake. Three or four other cars of questionable vintage followed closely behind with the rest of the workers.

We watched the men pile out and prepare the place to their liking with the shearing machine placed on a wooden platform. The machine has eight drops, four on either side, and is powered by the engine of a converted truck. Years ago men worked with hand shears such as are now used to trim shrubs. Next came clippers with a head similar to the ones barbers cut hair with but manually operated. The converted truck, with its complicated arrangement of belts and wheels, is a great improvement over these old methods which were both slow and back breaking.

The shearers stand ready; the goats wait in their pens on either side of the platform for the machine's engine to be started. As soon as the motor fires, each man grabs a goat by the hind legs, throws it to the floor, and holds it there while reaching for the nearest drop and beginning to clip. In minutes a fresh shorn goat is released, the fleece bundled and ready to be sacked, while the shearer reaches for the next victim.

Seeing these men at work is like watching a good show. The "bagger" is a happy little man, with more energy than intellect, who crawls into the bowels of the large sack looking like a tiny mole burrowing deep into a hole. He executes a little dance as he stomps and packs down the contents. The "tacole" boy is kept busy dabbing his thick, black gooey salve on the nicks and cuts left by the clippers.

The cook is the one I am especially interested in for I like the kind of coffee he serves.

"Jack," I asked one day, "do you think it would be all right if I go over to their camp for a cup of coffee?"

"Of course it will," he answered. "They'll be pleased to have you. I drop in often. Once I ate some of their cabrito and it was the best I ever put in my mouth."

So, tying my horse, I climbed over the fence and approached the cook with, *"Una taso de cafe, por favor."*

The old man beamed from ear to ear as he picked up a large tin cup, dipped it into boiling water before pouring the brew. He gave it to me with one hand while the other held out a can of condensed milk.

The drink was fresh, hot, and good. I thanked him, untied my horse, and rode back to where the cowboy waited.

"Well," he inquired, "how was it?"

"Fine, but there was something about it that was very different. Sort of a sweetish taste," I told him.

"That?" He chuckled as he explained, "Have you never tasted Mexican coffee before? They always put the sugar and grounds together before adding water."

"So that was it. Well, I thought it was good and will be going back again."

The shearing crew's trip to the ranch in February is to "roof" the Angora nannies. It doesn't take them long to clip the hair from the head, legs, and under belly, leaving a protective cover over their backs. The purpose of this is both to allow the kids to get their milk fresh rather than strained through heavy, often dirty and matted, hair and also to permit the expectant mothers to range freely. We get a better kid crop doing this than clipping all the hair and keeping the mothers confined in a small area.

Slick goats, those that have been freshly shorn, have to be watched very closely for a rain or cold wind will cause them to chill down.

Any rancher who has dealt with Angoras knows that nature failed to supply them with a super abundance of sense. That old saying, "Goats don't have sense enough to come in out of the rain" is true.

The shearers make return trips in April and in September to remove all the hair from all the 'goras. Then, for six weeks, we must keep a watchful eye on the weather. Every afternoon some-one is out in the pasture collecting these naked or bald critters and driving them to a low, squat shed to spend the night. When the weather is threatening, it is necessary to herd them during the day, keeping close to the shed. The slightest patter of rain causes these weather sensitive creatures to bunch up. Huddled together in an effort to keep warm, they refuse to move but, crawling under or over each other, will stay in one spot until they smother or freeze.

A clap of thunder or flash of lightning interrupts any other activity during this post goat shearing surveillance period.

I have seen my husband jump up from his noonday meal and run for his horse at the first dim hint of approaching rain. He reacts in the same manner if an ominous looking cloud suddenly appears. I've known him to get out of bed at four in the morning, when he hears rain, and streak for the shed to see if any stragglers have been left out. Occasionally some that have been missed will follow in by themselves only to find the gate shut. Once Jack found thirty head huddled outside the pen when a cold rain and accompanying high wind sneaked in during the night. True to form, they refused to move and the man had only one alternative. He picked them up, one by one, and carried them into the shelter. Even so, some of the weaker ones nearly died, and the cowboy spent the rest of the night rubbing their numb legs to restore circulation.

I thought I was going to have a sick husband on my hands when I saw how tired and wet he was, but, after a hot breakfast and change of clothes, he was back in the pasture making certain others were not left out.

We were lucky and didn't lose a single goat but another rancher lost five hundred, chilled down by that same drenching rain and wind storm.

Experiences such as this prove how true that statement is that, "You may be a millionaire in goats today and a pauper tomorrow." Someone said, "It only takes a bucket of water and a palmetto fan to freeze out all the Goras in Kimble County."

Another rancher boasted once that he was the only man in the county not to lose any goats in a certain onslaught of severe weather. When asked to what he contributed his good luck, he replied, "Because I didn't have any of the crittters on my place."

The natural instinct of Angoras to crawl under or on top of each other is something they are born with and which we fail to take into consideration when we see them self-destruct. It isn't enough that they receive all the care given the other stock but we have to go further and protect them from themselves.

Spanish goats, on the other hand, are the least domesticated of all the stock because they require the least amount of coddling. They can endure almost all kinds of weather, are prolific breeders, and survive on practically nothing but acorns, leaves, weeds, and grass.

Getting them into a pen and holding them there is a different story. It requires a well constructed fence for they climb like monkeys, crawl like spiders, run like deer, and can disappear like magic.

Goats of this breed are basically loners and keeping them bunched in a herd is hard to do. Sometimes, as they are being driven toward the corral, a few will sneak into a clump of bushes and hide. As the others are drifted forward, the culprits will turn and run off, generally in the direction from which they came. One will be driving some 250 or 300 head and, looking back over his shoulder, spy 18 or 20 heading for a ravine at a fast trot.

Fortunately, we do not round them up but twice a year. Once they are securely penned, they get the works: drenched, vaccinated, castrated, branded, culled, and subjected to their semiannual DDT bath. All the ranch stock gets sprayed twice a year and occasionally some of the laborers are also sprayed.

When the kids are hatching, a ride in the pasture is similar to going on an Easter egg hunt. These precious babies: brown and white, white and black, black and brown, or solid colors can be found hidden under branches, behind rocks, or on cliff ledges. They lie there, cuddled up in a ball, head tucked close to the ground, and seeming to be asleep. Just get off your horse to approach one and it will be up and off, skipping and hopping like a jack rabbit.

Since the Spanish goats are so seldom disturbed, we find very few orphaned kids. There is nothing, though, more lovable and mischievous than one of them raised as a Sancho. Watching them jump on the hood of a parked car, looking at themselves in the windshield, and slide down the fender is a real joy. They can hold your attention for hours as they play with their improvised toys.

One of these orphans can prove invaluable when raised as a pet and trained to be a lead goat. Many of the truckers, specializing in hauling livestock, carry their own lead goat to help with the loading and unloading.

Alfalfa, our pet, is a great help around the pens. He has been taught to walk through gates, into a truck, or down the cutting chute and wherever he goes the rest of the stock follows. He steps out like a Majordomo and accomplishes more in a few minutes than we can, alone, in hours. When working with just us he is willing and helpful but he sulks whenever asked to perform with a trucker's goat. He appears to be disdainful of the intruder and, as Jack complains, becomes "as stubborn as a goat."

CHAPTER 6

It was several years after our marriage that the REA brought electricity to our door. Before that we cooked on a wood range, read by lamp light, hauled ice from town, and warmed by the fireplace. Our telephone was the kind that you cranked to get central and every family on the line had a separate ring. Ours was one long and two shorts. There were times after a storm when the line would go dead because a tree had blown over or a wire had snapped. When that happened, the rancher was responsible for following the line through his property and repairing the break. Sometimes an ordinary piece of bailing wire could get the job done.

There are certain advantages, as well as disadvantages, to a party line. It can circulate news which is not always accurate, help locate a person, give advice, or sound an alarm. I was shocked at first to learn that people actually listened to others conversations and then talked about what they had heard, but I soon learned it was the accepted procedure.

We had a darling little old lady on the line who took the receiver off the hook every time the phone rang. She didn't pull any punches but came right out and said, "I heard Mr. Dixon tell Archie —" or she would ask, "Did you know that Eddie Allen was killed last night in a car accident?" The admirable part was that her inquisitiveness was always employed in a constructive manner. Never once was she known to repeat a bit of unsavory gossip.

She was comforting and helpful and, more than once, she and her hobby proved beneficial.

There was the time she heard a young mother, unable to locate the family physician, asking the operator to try to find him for her baby was choking on something and she didn't know what to do.

"Just hold him by the heels with his head down for a few minutes," came the sweet calm voice of experience. "If that does not work, you'll have to run your finger down his throat. Just remember to give him something warm to drink afterwards."

The same dear soul came to our assistance once when she overheard me tell Peggy that one of our horses had a severe cut and Jack was unable to get the bleeding stopped.

"Tell him to pour a bottle of finger nail polish in the cut," was her advice.

Someone told the story about tricking a listener who hogged the line and exaggerated her information. The lady doing the talking, knowing she was being overheard, said to her friend, "I smell beans burning. Don't you?" and there was the responding sound of the receiver clicking as it was hung up.

Our telephone system fascinated my little nine-year-old cousin who had come out from the city for a weekend visit. He had been in the room near the phone for some time before re-marking, "The guy with one ring surely gets a lot of calls."

"What?" I asked him. "Who gets a lot of calls?" Then it registered.

I told my husband about his remark after we had gone to bed, and he had a good laugh. "Doesn't the crazy kid know that is how we contact the operator? Wonder what he would do if he had to put through a call? Stand there all day with the receiver in his hand?"

We were amused again the next morning when he went with Jack to the barn. Standing there beside the man as he was milk-ing, the youngster's curiosity got the better of him and he pointed to the cow and asked, "Which one is for chocolate milk?"

Going to town is an announcement, which draws errands like ants to butter. The neighbors start calling, "I hate to bother you but would you mind getting —?" The shopping list gets long-er every time the phone jingles. One particular day the requests weren't many and I nearly always visited the same shops on my

20

trips in. I was asked to go by Loefflers to see if a tire had come in, by the post office for a COD package, by Josephs for some thread, and Holekamps for vaccine.

My own personal list, which I found not long ago in a sweater pocket, read:

Light bill	$8.75
Car license	$16.50
Laying pellets	100 lbs.
Kerosene	50 gals.
Laundry	take and pick up
Flour	25 lbs.
Potatoes	Large sack
Nipples	
Salt	10 blocks
Anthrax vaccine	100 doses
Cokes	take empties
Seeds	variety

Jack takes fiendish delight in telling about some of my disastrous shopping expeditions and even sets traps for me. We had been planning a garden and discussing the seeds we needed so, as I was leaving the house, he reminded me to get the seeds, especially the macaroni.

Checking my list at the store, I asked for the seeds.

"Mac — aa — roni —?" stammered the clerk, his face getting redder and redder, his cheeks puffing. He disappeared to the back from where I distinctly heard roars of uncontrolled laughter.

On one occasion I asked that same man to help me find a certain brand of vegetable. I was searching for Squibbs when I wanted Libbys. I never know how to buy bananas, tomatoes, or oranges. Is it by the number or pound? When fryers were on sale for forty-five cents, I couldn't understand why I was charged a dollar fifteen for a two and a half pound chicken.

Eventually, that clerk and I became very good friends. His name is Lester, and he is actually the owner. He is a jolly individual with a big belly like Santa Claus, which shakes when he laughs. He is also a dyed in the wool Democrat and told me once that "When the Republicans were in office the last time, the people in Kimble County were so poor they had to use prickly pear for toilet paper."

21

CHAPTER 7

People everywhere enjoy a change. Just getting away from the everyday mode of life gives them a lift, and going to the country is a very special way of doing this. It enables one to shake off worries like a hound dog shakes off water. "Going to Grandma's" has been a fun vacation for families for years, and, while we aren't grandparents, the warmth of our hospitality is just as comforting. Many of our friends often drive out for a change.

Leaving behind the stink of diesel, the hustle and bustle, the discord of city noises is like stepping out of a tight pair of shoes at the end of day.

Our house is spacious and comfortable, food generous, and entertainment á la carte.

Capt. Ben Syllivan, who was stationed at Fort Sam Houston, and his wife had just stopped their car late one afternoon and were in the act of getting out when we heard Jack calling. He had let the boys go to town and was at the barn doing the chores.

"Bring a flashlight and shotgun," he called.

"Shotgun?" the captain asked. "What do you suppose he wants with it?"

"Don't know," I replied, "but I'll get them. Do you want to go with me?"

We heard it long before we reached the barn. The hissing, sizzling, clattering of a rattlesnake coiled and ready to strike. The buzzing tune played by tiny buttons on the end of his tail can paralyze one with fear. It sends cold chills to the heart of the

22

bravest of men. This is a tune which means business and demands respect.

I held the flashlight while Jack shot. His greeting to Ben, who had just seen his first rattlesnake, was to cut off the rattlers and hand them to him. Jack acted as though that was all in a day's work but I could see signs of nervousness and understood why when he explained to us what had happened.

The feed for the milk cow is kept in an abandoned hen house. A hole, approximately ten inches square, had been cut in the bottom of the door to permit chickens to come and go, and it was there, just inside that hole, that the snake was coiled. Hearing the rancher approach, the snake had sounded its musical warning.

At least it had played fair.

Snakes of every kind haunt abandoned houses, wood piles, and caves. They also like the warmth of midday when they lie, napping, on stock trails, old wagon roads, exposed roots of trees, or rocks. Unsuspecting animals searching for fresh grazing are frequently bitten on the nose or neck. These bites, though painful, are seldom fatal. Horses become suspicious after being bitten, shying at twisted sticks, shadows, or the rustling of dried weeds.

Chickens, too, dislike snakes and huddle together, clucking or squawking until the entire barnyard is put on the alert. Just any kind of reptile disturbs them. Bull, coachwhips, or chicken snakes are the most troublesome for they live in woodpiles or under sheds and feed on rats and eggs.

Chickens are not alone in being annoyed by these pests for I have had my share of scares. A few times when I have been careless, not looking before reaching into a nest, my hand has contacted with a wet, slimy, squirming object rather than the round, firm one I was expecting.

Diablo, a flea bitten gray horse, can smell rattlers. He had been left up in the pen one night and, when Jack started toward the barn the next morning, was standing near the door, snorting and pawing. A large rattlesnake lay just inside, coiled and sleeping.

Perhaps the most terrible experience of my life was the time I was standing at the sink and heard Maria screaming to me for help. Her little two-year-old son had just been bitten on his foot as he played next to their house.

I wrapped my dishtowel around his leg as a tourniquet, grabbed the car keys and straightened out the road to Junction.

That must have been the longest and fastest ten miles anyone ever drove. Frantically I searched both sides of the road for a patrol car but none ever showed. The doctor, at least, was in his office and immediately made an incision and applied suction. Then he took us to the hospital for further treatment and care.

Doctors, technicians, nurses drifted in and out of the room like shrouded ghosts, doing all that they knew to do. Yet that wasn't enough. We were lost and trapped in a mass of nothingness. An ominous shadow seemed to hang over the threshold as though keeping our prayers from reaching God. We were numbed and chilled by a hard, cold fear.

Five o'clock the next morning, the nurse closed little Johnny's eyes and straightened his body. She and I stood, side by side, and looked at the plump, cuddly legs and saw that they were both alike. There was no swelling on the left one where the snake had struck him. He, I have always thought, died from shock not from the poison of the snake. But what difference does it make? He was gone.

Early the next morning, the Mendozas drove slowly out the gate. A little white coffin rested on the back seat as the car started on its way to Old Mexico.

Years ago, my mother and I attended a funeral service in an African American church for a little girl, the granddaughter of our family cook. The minister had an elegant delivery and a masterful command of word as he sketched a picture of God's garden. I can't recall his exact words but they were something like: "Most of the flowers in the Heavenly garden were wilted and dead, their petals shedding and falling. That day there would be a beautiful, perfect bud on the bush. The life which had just departed would bring fresh joy to the angels."

With Johnny's death, another bud would appear in the Garden.

CHAPTER 8

It was late in October and Autumn had just made her official entrance clad in a cool, dark misty gray ensemble. She wore no accessories, not even a single ray of sunshine, to brighten the somberness of her costume. Our moods, too, were in accord with that of nature's for we were in the second year of a drought with range grasses gone, hay scarce, and the stock market flooded. Fortunately there was still the prickly pear to fall back on.

Ordinarily the lowly growth is considered a menace. Just knock off a leaf and it will immediately spawn many more of its kind. The plant resembles a cluster of hotcakes stacked edge to edge and generously sprinkled with assorted spikes. Each spike can stab far into the flesh of man or beast if touched, but cattle, sheep, and goats like to eat the succulent leaves when the thorns are removed.

It is quite a sight to see the stock savoring these juicy morsels, licking the escaping drops with long slobbering tongues. Luckily the feast is as good for them as it is to taste and miraculously puts pounds on their backs and nutrition in their milk.

To remove the thorns, the plant is set on fire. The thorns burn away leaving the pears. Stock will follow the men who set those fires and bite into the luscious pear-cakes while still warm or stand around chewing contentedly.

Today we use burners with the nozzle attached to a long hose connected to a butane tank which is mounted in the back of a truck. The fifty- to seventy-five-foot hose permits the men to cover a relatively large area. This is a definite improvement over the old way when each man carried a small kerosene tank strapped to his back.

One afternoon Pedro and Juan were on opposite sides of the truck as they walked about looking for a plant to attack. With flames spurting from the nozzle, each man was intently watching the thorny spikes sizzle and disappear and looked up just long enough to locate another clump. An exceptionally large and healthy looking cluster, growing among the protruding branches of a fallen tree, had caught Pedro's attention. Suddenly he stopped, stood as in a daze, looking at a strange object near his feet.

"Juan," he called. *"Ven per aqui. Mira. Que es?"*

Juan stepped to his side, looked at the object which was in front of him and shook his head, saying, *"Valgame, Dios! Yo no se. Sitamos ablarla el Petron."* Juan was as puzzled and frightened as Pedro and they finally agreed that Juan's suggestion was the thing to do. They would have to get the rancher to come and look. Then the question was whether they should wait until quitting time or go right away. Finally it was decided that Juan would stay to guard the find while Pedro went for the boss.

Juan obtained enough courage, while waiting, to stoop down and look at the thing more closely. Silver coins of all denominations and copper cents lay scattered in wild array among the interesting papers. Yellow, green, and red colored squares blossomed profusely amid the envelopes. Some of the colored bits of paper had escaped only to be held captive on the spikes of the large pear guarding the spot.

In a seemingly short time, important appearing people began to gather at the scene. There were local law enforcement officials, postal service employees, members of the FBI, and a Texas Ranger.

They all stood in a group while a middle aged woman, who had arrived with her husband, walked toward a small iron safe, its bottom beaten out, which lay at their feet. The profusion of coins, U.S. stamps, and legal documents told of the importance of the cache.

One of the postal service men held out a pair of rubber gloves to the woman, saying, "It is no doubt too late for finger prints but we can try," and he squatted down and began handing the papers to the woman.

The safe had been stolen some months before from the little post office in the back of the Segovia Country Store, owned and operated by Mr. and Mrs. Frank Hatch, where she was Postmistress.

Juan and Pedro, who had been standing there all the time were apprehensive with fear. Unable to understand anything that was said, they looked at the facial expression of the officers whose scrutinizing eye occasionally glanced in their direction. Even Jack had said something, indicating them.

That apprehension quickly disappeared when someone thought to collect the loose change and award it to them. With smiles on their faces they returned to work, pausing occasionally to jiggle the coins in their pockets and scan the surface hoping to make another discovery amid the prickly pear.

CHAPTER 9

It was one of the coldest days in October when the sheriff and his deputy were left handcuffed to a tree in our pasture.

To gather the sheep out of that pasture, we had started at daylight so we could pick them up on their bed grounds. The task of holding that bunch close to the fence while drifting toward the corrals had fallen to me, while the others fanned out, looking for more.

We made a good run and had them penned and counted by 9:30. One of the boys had just shaken and emptied a bottle of drench into the bucket and I was stirring it so failed to notice the two men walking rapidly toward us.

Jack, though, had gone to meet them and almost immediately the three men jumped into the pickup and rushed to the house.

Had I been blessed with even a reasonable amount of curiosity I would never have been so indifferent to my surroundings. It took a remark from one of the helpers to arouse my interest and stimulate action.

"Wonder what is wrong? Their scabbards are empty," said one of the men.

"Yeah! And did you see the handcuffs on the little guy?" asked the other.

Empty scabbards! Dangling handcuffs! That was enough to arouse anyone's curiosity. Mine was certainly activated as I mounted my horse and looped up the road.

One of the officers was talking over the phone as I entered the house. I soon learned that the two had been forced, at gun point, to drive through the night, been marched into the pasture where they were handcuffed to the tree. An arm of one was placed in the fork of an intertwining limb and secured to the arm of the other. Then, taking their pistols with him, their captor had walked away promising to return and release them when he had completed his mission. His mission was to go into Junction where his sister and brother-in-law lived, kill the man against whom he had a personal grudge.

The City Marshall had understood the urgency of the situation and promised that he and his deputies would go directly to the home. He added that he only hoped they could get there in time.

Luck was with them, as we were to learn later, for the husband was away on a trucking assignment. The intruder told his sister he would wait, pulled up a chair, and sat down with his gun across his lap.

I fed the men hot coffee and cookies while Jack went into the bedroom and came back with his old Colt .45. "Here," he said as he handed the gun to the sheriff, "You may need this."

While they gulped the hot coffee, the sheriff removed the handcuffs from his deputy's arm. We saw, then, how they hand managed to free themselves.

A little gold pocket knife, worn as a watch fob, which the older man's wife had given him as a Christmas present had done the trick. She must have been a very happy woman when learning that the little gift, used as a screwdriver, had probably saved her husband's life.

Sitting there at the table I made the statement that it was a good thing the wind had been out of the south that morning, otherwise I might have drifted the sheep by them.

"Lady," exclaimed the deputy, "we can all thank our lucky stars that you didn't ride by there while he was near. We would all have dead chickens. That baby meant business."

Talking about their ordeal on the way to town, one of them said, "You read about people being forced to do things at the end of a gun and wonder why they didn't do something. It is a different story when the gun is on you. I never thought a thing like that could happen to me."

29

The City Marshall had slipped through the back door and got the drop on the would be murderer where he had fallen asleep in the chair. We learned later that the man was indicted on four counts and sent up for twenty years.

The next week we received a copy of the *Mineral Wells Index*, dated October 9th. It read: SUSPECT LOCKS SHERIFF, AIDE TO TREE. Sheriff Fred Forman and Deputy Buddy Baker were taken on a 250 mile ride at the point of a 30-30 rifle, starting at two-thirty Thursday morning and, at the end of the trip, they were handcuffed to a tree and left stranded ten miles south of Junction.

CHAPTER 10

The hunters have returned for another season. They go into pastures and fields, surround watering places, hide in tree tops in pursuit of game. With bated breath they scan the distant horizon for a glimpse of that proud, antlered beauty stalking the timid doe.

This is a time of apprehension for we know the disastrous results which so often accompany the too eager itching of the trigger finer. Illegal deer, sheep, cattle, horses, even men have fallen victim to the over zealous marksman. While the take is excessive in game and human life, the county's financial gain is even greater.

The excitement of hunting, like that of most sports, is contagious. The very air seems to feel the stimulation. The enthusiasm even affects Jack and me. Days before the opening of the season, he gets out our guns, oils and sights them in. When I see him doing this, I remember the lists Dad would make.

The scribbling we would find on assorted bits of paper scattered about his desk revealed what he was thinking. We'd read:

bacon	canned milk	flour
eggs	molasses	etc.
potatoes	beans	

I'm certain the thrill I get out of hunting is a carryover from my childhood. Born in September, my parents took me on their annual hunt in November. That was in the horse and buggy days, and, because of the distance, we usually stayed a week or ten days. We traveled in a covered Studebaker wagon with a third horse tied to the back of it.

The yearly outing gained in novelty and comfort with the advent of the automobile but not in excitement. Brush country deer are larger and harder to find than are those of the Hill Country but their trophy antlers make it all worthwhile.

Jack gets his the easy and quick way. He walks them up and shoots, fast and true, at the running animal. I'm too slow and deliberate for that. I select a spot near a pass or feeding area and hide in a clump of brush to wait. The joy of the hunt, to me, is to affiliate with the pacific grandeur of nature as I sit on a tree stump or boulder.

This sitting and waiting method develops one into a competent woodsman. I've learned to look in the direction from which a bird, disturbed by the presence of a strange object, has flown. Squirrels will twitch their tails and bark to show anxiety. Another deer is coming when a grazing doe lifts her head, looks, flips her tail and resumes eating. The snap of a twig, falling leaf, or rock rolling, sounds an alarm. It is astonishing how small creatures like wood rats, lizards, or armadillos can create jarring discords by interrupting nature's symphony of silence.

Listening to the silence is one of my favorite pastimes. It reminds me of Malthia D. Babcoek's poem:

> This is my Father's world
> And to my listening ears
> All nature sings
> And around me rings
> The music of the spheres.

But there in the vast vacuum of space the wind breathes timidly against one's ears as if not wanting to disturb a single filament of hair. The rustling of fallen leaves is a rancorous medley of music. A sparrow's chirp comes loud and startling clear from across the ravine. Small rocks rolled by the scampering feet of a chipmunk echo with a thunderous rumble. A butterfly looms large as a hawk when fluttering among the branches. In the quiet stillness, the elements seem afraid to breathe as the clouds drift so slowly, so softly by.

My method of hunting is both pleasant and nerve racking. There have been so many times when, surrounded by does and

32

fawns, I have been literally forced to hold my breath for fear they would see me and warn off the wily bucks. I revel in the challenge to match wits with these creatures of the wild. When they become suspicious, perhaps from winding me, they will walk around with nostrils extended, white tail held high, stomp a foot and even emit a shrill whistle-like alarm. If I am clever enough and can refrain from moving until their curiosity is appeased, they will resume their grazing.

An unsuspecting buck walks with studied grandeur within range. Aroused to action, I must maneuver myself into shooting position. Slowly, ever so slowly, my heart pounding so hard and fast it nearly breaks my eardrums. I ease back the hammer of my 30-30 Winchester, take careful aim and remember to squeeze the trigger. When the shot goes wild, which it so often does, I am secretly relieved but when my mark falls, I am proud and pleased. Of course I have to stop and shed tears for the victim which, just a few seconds ago, was a warm and vigorous beauty who is now turning cold and stiff.

The cowboy was in a hurry one morning as he was returning from checking the camp of some hunters who had come in during the night. They couldn't resist taking a shot at a young buck which ran across the road in front of him. When the deer fell, he just grabbed it and threw it in the trunk of the car. The boys waiting at the corrals heard the knocking and bumping but were surprised when they lifted the lid to see a deer jump out and run off, only slightly stunned from where the bullet had struck its horn.

A wounded deer is dangerous. One charged the horse a neighbor on the Pflueger ranch was riding and, when the rider fell off the bucking and frightened horse, turned on the man. His wife called for help when the horse came in alone but the man was not found until after sunup the next day, bleeding from the many cuts and with a broken leg.

The sport of hunting is not the killing but the chase and the aftermath. We thoroughly enjoy visiting with our hunters in the evening as we gather around their campfire. Sitting there, beneath a star-studded sky in November, listening to and sharing stories and experiences with friends makes one realize that it is the simple things in life which make it all worthwhile.

CHAPTER 11

Jack thinks that one of the smartest moves he ever made was switching to Black Angus cattle. They are healthier, do not need to be dehorned, fatten more easily, and raise sturdy calves. He says that the time spent working with cattle has been cut in half with this switch.

This rancher husband of mine is old fashioned in morals and opinions and likes to do things the old way which, sometimes, is the hard way. Cattle branding is one of the few remaining ranch activities that is a carryover from the frontier days. Today, just as it did a century ago, the branding iron glows in a bed of red hot coals fanned by a blue flame before being applied to the calf's hide. A sickening stench of singed hair accompanies the cry of the protesting victim.

We have a squeeze chute, but it is never used when altering the bull calves. When the time comes for this, they are separated and thrown in the holding pen. Then, while the workers take a break to roll a smoke, Jack tests the sharpness of his knife. They all squat on their heels in a little huddle, laughing, smoking, and dreading the work ahead. I occupy myself by checking to see that we have everything that will be needed.

These Black Angus calves are salty little devils, and the men handling them had better know their business. An inexperienced helper runs the risk of being injured or of getting someone else hurt. There is an art to throwing a calf similar to that used by a roper in the arena but we use two men in the corral. One grabs the youngster by the nose, the other by the flanks. They lift and throw it down on the left side, holding the right hind leg out away from the body. The testicles are removed and swabbed with tac-ole; blackleg and penicillin shots are given at the same time.

A group of people were standing on the other side of the fence once and we heard one of the ladies say, "Oh, look! They're going to give the little darling a shot to deaden the pain. Isn't that sweet?" I never fill a syringe without remembering her remark. Wonder what her reaction would be to mountain oysters?

These newly made steers will eventually end up in the feeding lot, where there will be nothing for them to do but eat. There they will remain until they weigh a little over four hundred pounds and are shipped to market. There is money in the making if the rancher is good enough to estimate the weight accurately and not permit the animal to put on too much fat. A few pounds over the peak and the price falls.

Heifer calves have a happier prospect. They, too, must be branded, vaccinated, sprayed, but then they are left alone until old enough to be bred.

There is no peace and quiet for ranch families during wean-ing time. Cows take the privilege of being mothers very seriously and are emotionally upset when their offspring are taken from them. It really makes us sad to see them standing at the fence, sometimes for days and days, bawling as though their hearts are broken. The youngsters are just as bad and do their share of pleading to be returned to the loved ones.

The pastures are marked like checkerboards with dry cows, heifers, bulls, steers, and mothers all in different areas.

There are ever so many mouths to be fed every day that Jack feels it is necessary to explain when hiring a new man. "You will have to work every day, even on Sundays and holidays. The stock doesn't know any difference in their eating habits."

It isn't always required that we supplement the natural graz-ing but when those times do occur, the work load is very heavy. It usually comes at the end of winter when freezing weather has sapped all the nutrition out of the grasses or during the intense summer heat or during a drought. The men are not all that feel the crunch when supplementary feeding time is at hand for it is then the pickup sees double action. Since it is used to transport everything to the feeding areas, the sound of it coming down the road is recognized by the animals. Cattle will start bawling when they hear it; sheep and goats begin to gather at the grounds. After a few days of this service, they will be waiting when they hear it as if to say, "We have a date."

Bales of hay are piled high on the important conveyance and distributed to the horses every other day. We start blowing the horn, once inside their pasture, and wait for them to come. It doesn't take them long to learn what that horn means and to come running when they hear it.

Frijole, one of the dogs, likes to ride along and he synchronizes his barking with the blowing of the horn. Once we tried just letting him do the calling and the horses came just the same.

CHAPTER 12

The day a plane crashed in the pasture and burned, all ranch work came to an end. The little Piper twin engine exploded on contact with the ground, sending flames soaring high as the sky. The pilot, by some miracle, escaped with minor injuries but our pasture wasn't so lucky. We were fighting that fire, which consumed some four hundred acres for almost four days.

The flames spread to a nearby cedar brake just waiting for excitement. Cedar makes a hot crackling fire and spurts sparks in every direction while filling the air with a thick, choking smoke which hovers closely overhead.

Men came from all around with shovels, water barrels, and feed sacks. Volunteer firefighters from Junction arrived with their ranch water tank and equipment, but the fire wasn't easily brought under control.

Some of the wives and neighboring ladies came to help me and we drove out to the site at dark with drinks and food for the men working there.

We marveled at the beauty of the ghastly sight. It looked like the lights of a large city seen at night from a hilltop as we approached. A closer view presented a spectacle of magnificent splendor outlined against the horizon. Most of the flames had been put out, but trees of red hot coals loomed as lighted sky scrapers then, as they toppled and crashed, millions of brilliant sparklers skipped over the ground. The crimson glow reflected against the low hanging smoke appeared as a great red tent covering the land.

Our menfolk were tired, and felt that the fire was contained. Many departed, but Jack and his crew decided to stay a little longer. About midnight the wind shifted to another direction, fanning the coals into a roaring inferno again.

Early the next morning bulldozers arrived and began clearing a large right-of-way to prevent the sparks from jumping. The wind, like an evil witch determined to destruct, changed directions a third time and sent the fire crawling out of the valley and up the hillside.

We felt, at the time, that it was a devastating loss but rains and warm weather brought tender weeds and new grass to cover the area, converting it into a grazing mecca. Here, at roundup time, could be found most of the stock enjoying themselves.

We had another experience with a plane landing, but the result was different.

Near the intersection of U.S. Highways 83 and 271 is a little roadside park not far from the entrance to the ranch. Jack and I were on our way to Junction, one day, when a small plane swooped down headed right at us. We pulled over to the side and watched as it landed. The wheels had barely touched the earth before the pilot was off and running towards the other highway where a small car stopped beside him. He talked for a few seconds with its occupants then returned to his plane.

I could scarcely believe my eyes as I watch the approaching man. Could it actually be who I though it was? Yes, for as he came nearer, a big grin popped out. The son of old family friends who had grown up across the street from us in San Antonio.

Steve explained to us, after we discussed the strange circumstances, that his wife, the driver of the small car, was on her way to California and had forgotten the certificate of title. She, and the friends with her, had stopped in Kerrville and then the arrangement was made for the meeting and for Steve to bring the title. It worked out just as planned and gave us a bit of excitement as well.

A few weeks later we had a surprise visit from my college roommate which was almost as exciting.

The war had placed such a ban on gasoline, new tires, and automobiles that a lot of people preferred to travel by bus, and it

38

was by bus that my roommate arrived in Junction. We, of course, knew nothing about the visit until she called from the bus station.

Bertha couldn't have picked a more inconvenient time for her surprise. A slow freezing rain had covered the Hill Country for three days with temperatures in the low twenties. A thin coating of ice draped the landscape and made the roads slippery and dangerous. The telephone was one of the few things that was working, and, when it rang, gave me a start. Hearing that she was in Junction did more than startle me.

"Hi, Connie. It's me, Bertha. I decided to give you and Jack a surprise visit and I'm in Junction. Can you come after me?"

"Well er — er, yes, but it will be a while for I don't have a way of getting in. I'll have to wait until Jack comes in at noon. Will you be all right?" I inquired.

"Sure!" she laughingly responded. "I'll be just fine."

And I knew she would. Not only was she an exceptionally good looking young woman but she had an effervescent personality. She could gather a crowd like honey collects bees.

The cowboy wasn't any better prepared to handle the situation than I when he came in. The roads had become so treacherous that he had abandoned the truck and borrowed a horse to get home. We decided the only thing we could possibly do was for me to ride the hose back to the truck and go in from there to pick her up.

Bertha called back shortly after I left the house and Jack told her that I was on my way but it would take a while since I was on horseback.

The honey had drawn the bees by the time I entered the station. Always something of an actress, my roommate had made a romantic mental picture of herself, dressed in traveling clothes, straddling a horse. Actually, I think she was just a little bit disappointed that it wasn't going to be that way.

CHAPTER 13

When I went to the barn one morning, after an unusually hard rain, I found my horse already saddled.

"What is this?" I asked. "It isn't my birthday."

I love the little grin that crinkled in the corner of my husband's mouth as he answered. "Yep! I know. But I er – er – have a favor to ask of you. We must finish this job here and I wish you would ride in the Neck for me. Just look around to see that all is well."

"Will do." I nodded. "I'd like to take one of the dogs with me, if you don't mind."

"Not at all," Jack said, approvingly. "That is a god idea. It will keep you company."

The Neck is an "L" shaped pasture bordered on one side by a rough ravine which is dry most of the time. Resting in a valley surrounded by many hills, this little arroyo becomes a raving maniac when angry runoff waters rumble and churn through its narrow canyon. In some places the banks are eight to twelve feet straight up and just wide enough for a horse and rider.

Today was one of those times when the rain had stimulated intense activity in this area of the pasture and I rode with extreme caution. It must have been about an hour later, as I skirted the edge of this boiling inferno of running water, that I heard the dog bark in a strange manner. I understood the excitement in his bark when I caught up to him.

There, in the clearing, was a little black calf struggling to stand erect on wobbly legs. I judged it to be two or three days old but why was it alone? The tracks made by the dog and calf were the only visible ones. Mother cows, especially those with baby calves, would have come running when hearing the barking dog.

A baby calf, alone, in a pasture in which I knew there were no cattle had me puzzled. We often find sheep or goats on the highway where they have been left by harassed truckers who, fighting against time to untangle a mass of crowded, smothering animals, had lifted them over the sides of the truck. The driver continues on his way either thinking the ones in the road were dead or he had simply forgotten them.

But a calf? No way!

What was I to do? I wasn't strong enough to hoist it on my horse, and I didn't have a piggin string with which to tie it. Go back and tell Jack about it was all I could think to do.

It took almost as long to convince the men that I wasn't joking as it did for us to get back to the calf.

The next morning the boys, riding the fenceline, found broken stays and hair on the wire but the rain had obliterated all tracks. The stockman thought that the calf, more than likely a twin, had been asleep when the cows grazed out of sight. When the infant awoke, it blindly staggered in the wrong direction.

Sancho, the Mexican name for orphan, is what we call the motherless animals we pick up and raise by hand. I once had twenty-five lambs and kids at the same time but this was to be my first calf. "Wonder" was the name which seemed most appropriate for her.

And I have always wondered why Jack asked me to ride that particular pasture that morning. Just what is this special power he has, this ESP, which enables him to ferret out problem spots? I have seen it put to the test time and time again.

"I'm going to ride in the 1300 this afternoon," he announced one day. True to form, he rode up on a heifer long in labor and, dismounting, assisted her to deliver a bull calf. She would have died without his help and strength.

Another time he postponed a trip to town to ride in the Dillingham. He found a horse standing with his legs braided between the wires. The horse had been there so long that his legs were numb, but, with a little cowboy assistance, circulation soon returned.

I have seen these hunches take him to pastures where stock waited beside empty troughs with broken floats; fighting bulls have knocked down a fence; goats cry to be released when their hair was caught in the grasp of a thorny bush. When one of the dogs disappeared, he found it with a snare, left by a trapper, around its neck.

Not only is the cowboy endowed with this apparent psychic instinct which controls his conduct in locating trouble, but he knows what to do when he finds it. How did he learn that mother cows would run to protect their young from a dog? How could he have been so quick in his response when, driving a herd of cattle across the highway, one refused to cross the yellow stripe in the center? His rope flashed and the loop settled across its neck and the steer was across the road almost all at the same time. There had been no hesitation in his action reflex.

When we returned home late one night from the movies, Jack drove straight to the barn. There, in the car lights, we saw our young stallion standing in a pool of blood, his chest laid open. While I held the flashlight, the rancher took thirty-three stitches which were so neat that, when the cut healed, no scar was visible.

How could he have known that the horses in the remudo would wander close to the pen and the stud, fighting with them, would snag his chest on the pickets? Normally, when returning late at night, we stop at the house.

In all our married years there was one situation when Jack didn't know what to do and I did. It was the time our little party line listener suggested using fingernail polish to control bleeding. My husband had tried it, and it had worked but left the residue of the varnish on his hands. He was trying to remove it with his pocket knife, getting off more skin than polish with the scraping, when I offered him my bottle of clear liquid and told him to wipe it on his hands and it would remove the polish.

CHAPTER 14

Sheep graze contentedly on today's ranges thanks to government trappers and wolf-proof fencing. There are still a few remote areas where watchdogs or guard donkeys are needed for protection against mountain lions or coyotes.

The first time we invade the privacy of the sheep is the second week in January. Then we see the shearers driving down the road again, but, as it was with the goats, their stay is short for they have come just to tag the ewes. Tagging is to sheep similar to roofing of goats except the wool is only clipped from their heads, legs, and genitals. This is done to allow the lambs to nurse sanitarily and comfortably and to prevent infection in the ewes.

The baby lambs start dropping in early February, and it isn't long after that we start marking. We must hire extra help because gathering and penning a bunch of ewes with babies is one of the most nerve-racking tasks the stockmen have to face. These frisky babies will follow anything that moves, including horses, dogs, even jackrabbits.

It isn't at all uncommon to see a gang of twenty or thirty baby lambs start running as though they are playing a game. When that happens, there is nothing a rider can do but stop and wait. Sometimes my husband has trouble getting the extra help to just stop and wait because the natural instinct is to try to head them off, which would work with the adults but not the youngsters.

Stopping and waiting is one of the many things Jack has learned from experience just as he has learned what to do when lambs start dying from Clabber Belly. Generally the largest and fattest lambs suffer from this condition which, apparently, comes from eating grass while still nursing. The cowboy thinks that the jousting about from being gathered and the letting of blood when marked is what corrects the problem.

Marking is another term for branding, but it also refers to a time when the lambs receive a lot of attention.

Jack stands with his back to the fence while the men pick up a lamb and stand facing him. They put its head between their legs and pull the hind legs far apart and against their chests. In this position it is easy for the stockman to castrate the males, but the females are merely cradled in the arms of the holder. Once the testicles are removed, the helper turns his back to the cowboy so the ear can be nicked and tail removed.

Our ewe lambs carry a swallow fork or "V" clipped out of their left ear and the muttons have the tip of their right ear cropped. I scratch each infant with sore mouth vaccine and the tacole boy dabs his miracle drug freely.

Children growing up on ranches know that the nursery rhyme: "Little Bo Peep has lost her sheep. Leave them alone and they'll come home, dragging their tails behind them" is not true for their tails are taken away from them at an early age.

We couldn't help but laugh when one of our hunters came by to tell us that he had seen a freak sheep in the pasture.

"You did!" Jack said in surprise. "What did it look like?"

"It had a long tail," was Maddox's explanation. "Must have been one we missed," was all Jack had to say, but he did take time to explain that he was very particular about removing all the lambs' tails.

There are a few other things that this cowboy husband of mine is particular about. Hats have to be Stetsons, jeans Levis, and his knife must be sharp. He carries a whet stone in his pocket all the time and uses it, almost from force of habit. Some men wear out a pocket with their Copenhagen, Jack does with his knife.

When the gate to the marking pen is thrown wide open and the greatly changed and now subdued lambs seek consolation from their mothers, I go to work.

On the ground, near where the cowboy's knife was so active, is a bloody, greasy mass of ear tips and assorted sizes of tails. I flop down in the middle of all this carnage and begin sorting the tails in piles of ten. Should I take time to look up, I would find all eyes on me. The laborers might be rolling their Bugler smoke, the extra help taking out their ready rolled, and Jack with his whet stone in action; all would be waiting for the outcome. Most of the times they will have a bet on the count. This particular time we had a total of 768 tails from the 778 ewes which were in the pasture. A very good percentage for that year's crop.

CHAPTER 15

Spring is the happiest and busiest time of the year. It is the time when the bitter cold winds of winter soften to become warm, caressing breezes. Then tender leaves sprinkle tree tops, and the baby calves, lambs, and kids trot beside their mothers. These new lives are a fulfillment of God's promise that there shall be everlasting life.

There is pleasure and wonderment in our hearts as we watch this miracle of birth. There is also awareness of our obligation to these newborn. Our work is cut out for us if we are to protect them from the devil.

The devil is not that traditional one seen in red tights with a pitchfork in his hand, but it is an innocent looking, almost inconspicuous little fly. We call him the "screw worm fly." He sails about depositing eggs in the tender navels of the newly born. He soars across the pastures searching for cuts, scratches, and sores upon which to feed.

You can easily detect these eggs if you look closely at the wound. At first glance you may think it only a white blob but closer scrutiny will reveal thousands of tiny pin points, or eggs, clustered in one minute spot. These tormenting insects show no partiality but attack indiscriminatingly, man or beast. The eggs hatch quickly, turning first into a seething, squirming mass of small white worms boring further into the flesh, sucking blood. As they dig deeper, they grow. It takes only a few short days for these maggots to complete their destruction. Stockmen find it necessary to hire extra help to conduct a crusade against these insidious murderers.

The cowboy was alone, except for his dog, the day he found the break in the fence. He saw the broken stays and the wire pulled from the posts and stretched into the next pasture. He also found traces of hair on the wires and fresh cow tracks. Ranchmen would make good detectives for they recognize fresh from old signs, know the type of animal involved and in which direction it was headed.

Jack read that these tracks were fresh and knew that they belonged to one of the registered bulls. He made a makeshift repair job on the fence and went in search of the truant animal. Driving the bull back to the gate, he made his first mistake. He dismounted, tied his horse, and walked back behind the sulking toro.

The innocent horse tied in front of it presented an inviting target to the truant animal which lowered its head, snuffed, pawed the ground, and charged. The cowboy, seeing the danger, ran toward his horse wildly waving his hat to divert the direction of the charge. The tactics worked, for the man, not the horse, became the object of attraction. It was then that a small bundle of black, barking hysterically, darted forward nipping and snapping at the attacking animal. This unexpected turn of events gave the man time to mount his horse and take command of the situation.

Protecting his horse was the cowboy's main objective, just as protecting his master was the dog's objective.

Jack knew he had made a careless mistake and endangered the lives of his horse, dog, and himself. So he spent extra effort in caring for the cut in the bull's side, where screw worms had already started their work of destruction.

Dogs are almost indispensable in our work although Jack was slow to acknowledge their value. Border collies are beautiful, graceful, friendly, and intelligent. They require very little training as the herding is an instinct. We have to keep our dogs tied when not in use. If we didn't, they'd have all the chickens gathered in a corner, and we would be without eggs. Dogs are so eager to work that, given a chance, they'll sneak into a pasture, find and hold sheep or goats in a bunch all by themselves. These dogs are graceful and quick, making it a pleasure to watch as they stalk their prey like a cat playing with a mouse.

Dogs and horses are the children we never had and hold a

special place in our hearts. We spend a lot of time working with and training these animals, and we take pride in the performance of the finished product.

We paid an unusually large stud fee to have our dog named Trouble bred and, like proud parents, eagerly awaited the blessed event. When the phase of gestation passed and the vet told us the dog had experienced a false pregnancy, we were naturally disappointed but resigned ourselves to accept it.

Some two weeks later a sound similar to that of a small puppy caught our attention. There, in the far recesses of Trouble's house, we found a round, squirming ball of curly black hair. Nature had handed us a welcome surprise.

That night a hard rain had pounded the country and left the morning with a blustery wind. Jack had planned a business trip to San Antonio but hated to leave the mother and pup without greater protection than that afforded by the doghouse. We thought they would be warmer in the hay barn, so we moved them there before we left.

The trip didn't take too long and the first place we went upon returning was the barn. Trouble met us at the door, but there was no sign of her puppy. It was still cold outside and very dark as we searched. Then, from somewhere, Jack heard the faint cry and knew the baby was alive. Fifty bales of hay had to be moved before we could retrieve the puppy from where it had fallen.

"Toughie" seemed to be a good name for a little fellow who could survive such a tumble. And he lived up to his name, making the best dog Jack ever had. When friends would ask my husband how much his dog was worth, he'd answer: "Fifty bales of hay."

CHAPTER 16

The man I married is without any fancy trimmings. He has never crossed a college campus nor walked down the dark, impressive halls of an administration building. The Ph.D. he holds is from the College of Common Sense.

While most men make the laws, Jack keeps them. No one has, nor could, question his honesty or integrity. When he says he'll meet you at 9:00, he'll be there at 8:55, come hell or high water. Doing a job halfway, taking the light end of the load, and crossing a street in the middle of the block are qualities alien to his character.

Jack was born and reared in the country, attend a one-teacher school, and was never out of the country until he was nineteen.

The best way to understand this man is to turn back the pages and look at him as a little boy. He was the only son and the eldest of seven children. There were always too many mouths to feed and not enough money. The family lived in a four-room house on the edge of their one-hundred acre farm. The discomfort of their crowded quarters was aggravated by the lack of electricity and indoor plumbing. The mother worked over a wood stove and washed clothes with water pulled up in a bucket from the rain cistern on the back porch.

The rear door opened out on two well-worn paths. One path led to the barn, the other to a little two-seater outhouse hidden demurely in a clump of shiny oak trees.

Members of the family look back today on their early home

life and marvel at the contentment they shared growing up together. The mother always had time for her children, even when all of her work was done by hand. Their father, too, was kind and understanding.

Their home was on the banks of Verde Creek where many years of flooding spread fertile bottom soil over their land. Still, it was a constant struggle to make ends meet. The father labored with his financial problems like a drowning man fights the water —his head above but his feet mired down as though tied with a rock. The two mules, once slick and fat, now plodded along on weak and shapeless legs, keeping rhythm to the flopping of their long ears. The harness, which hung on their lean backs, fitted them no better than it conformed to the fence over which it was thrown at midday. The old man behind the plow seemed to be following, rather than guiding, it as he walked with an air of dejection and defeat. Back and forth, up and down, row after row, the trio wound their slow, methodical way until the sun was high over head. With the team unhitched and watered, the man walked slowly into the house for his own lunch.

Wiping his mouth with a shirt sleeve, he shoved the plate to the center of the table and pushed back his chair. Laboriously he leaned over, unlaced his shoes, and padded to the front door where he stretched out flat on the floor. The bare boards were cool to his aching back and, in no time at all, the tired man was fast asleep.

Father was resting. The entire household must be quiet. The youngest children were sent out into the yard and cautioned to play in the shade of the gnarled mulberry tree. Their mother gently stirred the coals in the stove and placed some wood chips and a few twigs to start up the fire. She dropped the bucket gently into the well, poured the fresh water into the dishpan, and, while the water was heating, removed the dishes from the table.

Her husband stirred and stretched as she was wiping out the dishpan and started to hand out the towel to dry. Getting to his feet slowly, he laced his boots, drew a cool drink, and reached for his hat. From where he stood, he could see the mules with their necks across each others in mutual protection from the annoying flies. The constant stomping of feet and twisting of tails tippled the peaceful noontime lull.

Then Pa slammed the door.

A sudden awakening took place before the vibrant humming of the coiled springs ceased to quiver. Chickens started cackling, geese scolded, peacocks screamed, and the cow resumed her bawling for the calf. The children left their playhouse in the tree and ran into the kitchen, banging the door again and again. An old brown hound crawled out from beneath the house and trailed the man to the barn and laid down against the leaking trough to wait for the mules to be harnessed.

When the shadows had lengthened until they blended with the fading light, Ma held the gate open for Pa and his team. She had just turned old Jersey out in the trap and carried a bucket brimming with milk. The two moved with smoothness and confidence of years. Words were unnecessary as the weary woman and tired man completed their chores and walked toward the lighted lamp's glow beckoning to them.

Supper of hot biscuits and milk would be waiting for them by the time Father hung his hat on the deer antlers and washed his face and hand.

The little ones were sprawled on the floor, playing with their paper dolls when the screen door banged again and Jack, carrying an arm load of wood, walked in.

"You're late, son," his father said. "What kept you?"

"Yes, sir, I know. Had to help George hunt his cow before I could leave. Her calf came today and Old Bossie was hiding out with it." The explanation was made with his face half hidden in the towel with which he was wiping his face.

"What in heaven's name have you done to yourself?" inquired the concerned mother as she moved to get a better look at her son. "Have you been fighting again?"

What should he say? Should he tell her the truth? It wasn't easy for this ten-year-old boy, standing tall even then in his bare feet, to talk about his troubles. No amount of threatening or pleading could force him to empty his troubled heart to his parents. Some inner power warned the youth against causing them any additional worry. He knew that his father, hot-headed and unreasonable when disturbed, would not understand. What was a bloody nose and blackened eye in comparison to the defeated anguish of the adults?

All of this he weighed out in his mind before replying to his mother's question.

"We were just playing. It isn't half as bad as it looks. Gee, those biscuits sure smell good."

The youngster felt he was able to look after himself without involving his parents. The children of the affluent are often, through carelessness, cruel and inconsiderate of others. Their taunts and slights go so much deeper than they realize. The sensitive and less aggressive classmates suffer from these thoughtless slurs for the rest of their lives.

Jack, who had chores to do before and after school, who worked on Saturdays and Sundays also had the honor of his young sisters to defend. He took his responsibilities seriously and, while no troublemaker, his temper flared like a lighted firecracker when he felt they had been ridiculed.

One thing his good parents would never know was that the bloody nose and blackened eyes he carried home that night came as a result of a taunting cry, "Jack rides a jackass. Jack's ass rides a jackass to school. Which one is the donkey?"

Jack did ride a jackass to school. He rode that little donkey every day through all kinds of weather, and, his last year of school, his sister rode behind him on it. But, by that time, he had made certain the donkey was accepted as a proper mode of transportation. No one dared joke about, or tease him, anymore. The imprint of his protective influence was so strong that none of the six sisters ever felt humiliated or embarrassed when riding it.

Standing up for his rights was the seed of this boy's philosophy. Two of his uncles had died in World War I fighting for democracy, and, with that as his standard, he knew it his duty to demand respect. It was the value that he put on fair play which ultimately earned him the admiration and confidence of his playmates.

Awareness, even at an early age, of his obligation and of the financial burden carried by his father, prompted the boy to quit school and go to work.

Soon after quitting school he bought himself a horse. He had earned the money working with shearing crews, hay baling, and in road construction gangs where he drove a hitch of six horses. He plowed fields, ran a reaper, and milked cows for a dairy.

What the boy lacked in showmanship was easily augmented by the style and class of the little mare he purchased. She soon

52

proved a favorite at neighborhood matched races, a popular Sunday rural entertainment. People would come from miles around when the word got out that there was to be a gathering. They knew there would be jack pot roping and races followed by a box supper and dancing.

That little mare of Jack's was a good drawing card for she was faster than the best. The popularity of horse and rider attracted attention and soon men were asking the boy to work with their horses. When he wasn't roping a horse, he was riding one for fun at a rodeo. It was in this connection that he was brought to the attention of Col. W. T. Johnson, the originator of the World's Championship Rodeo now owned by Everett Colburn.

The colonel took his show to New York City every year for the month of October, and he asked Jack to go along. There the country boy gained recognition as a roper and trainer of horses. Mr. Johnson gave him year-round employment at one of his ranches, and Jack was on his way.

CHAPTER 17

Many of our friends have expressed surprise that Jack's and my marriage has been such a happy and successful one since our backgrounds are so unalike. When I hear this statement, I think of an experience I had as a child.

I stood on the muddy, chocolate-colored Rio Grande near where the crystal clear Devil's River emptied into it. For as long as the eye could see, these two rivers ran side by side, one clear blue, the other murky goo, before merging as one on their way to the Gulf of Mexico. All they had in common was water with a destiny awaiting.

All Jack and I had in common was horses. We were both exposed to these four-footed beauties at an early age. We learned to love and understand them with a dedication that would remain with us an entire lifetime. While Jack, as the eldest of seven children, had to work for everything he had, I was smothered with too much indulgence and attention.

I was born and grew up in the little Texas border town of Eagle Pass, where my parents, maternal and paternal aunts, uncles, and grandparents all resided and vied amongst themselves for my affection. What they got was the dregs of what affection was left after being lavished on the family pets.

Old pictures show Mother holding a smiling four month infant on the milk cow's back, while Dad, kneeling, manipulates the faucets which produce milk.

Every childhood picture shows a faithful dog somewhere

near and it was, perhaps, his protective care rather than that of the adults which permitted me to survive. Like the time he found me halfway across the International Bridge on my way to old Mexico, and, clutching the hem of my dress in his mouth, returned a reluctant four-year-old adventurer to the family bosom.

At the age of five, I was riding my own horse, courtesy of one of the doting grandfathers. When I was six, my father took me to the Indio Ranch on a large roundup and cattle drive. It was early morning when we left home in a heavy drizzle, which soon turned into an all day rain. Long before dark we found ourselves in the middle of a large laguna with no idea where the road went. We spent the night in the wagon and awoke the next morning to find water surrounding us in all directions. Dad, knowing there was no chance of locating the road, decided to abandon the wagon and go the rest of the way on the horses. It must have been about an hour later that we came upon a fence rider mending a water gap who pointed us in the right direction. The wagon was towed into camp about two days later.

I was proudly accepted as one of the gang and have always remembered that experience—especially one part of it. All of the cowboys were Mexicans and it was one of their customs which made the lasting impression on me. They have a custom of cooking the head of the calf being barbecued and giving the eyes to the men who have the best record of the day. It is quite an honor to be offered this choice morsel, and, out of kindness, they offered the prize to me one day. I really haven't enjoyed bar-b-que since.

Although my cowboy husband and I grew up in different environments, we both rode horses and, to this day, we still enjoy it. It isn't just the riding that we enjoy. It is the pride of possession and the pleasure we obtain from being able to understand the animals.

CHAPTER 18

"What kind of a husband does a cowboy make?" is a question I am asked many times.

If anything, I answer, "a better than average one." These men of the open range have long thought of the range as a man's world, calling for great stamina and endurance. They know the strength and courage sometimes needed to endure arduous conditions, and they feel that such a life could be unendurable for most women. Believing this, as they do, they acquire greater respect for their wife when she chooses to face the sacrifices of these conditions just to be with her husband.

I know that is how Jack feels about me, and, from what I have observed in the other husbands I have met, that is how they feel about their wives.

My husband is very protective and goes out of his way to make things easier for me. Before we were married he warned that his hours were long and he was sometimes confined to the ranch for indefinite periods. He painted a picture of household inconveniences due to lack of electricity, the presence of rattle-snakes, rabid coyotes, and other lurking dangers.

Conditions have improved greatly since then and a cowboy's wife, today has a much more comfortable life than did the pioneer woman who lived on the trail. She now has a substantial house to live in and stability in her day to day life. The man she lives with is, after all, just a normal person with all the traits and characteristics of any other man.

Kind and considerate as the cowboy is, he still has some qualities short of perfect. He invariably comes home at two o'clock when lunch is ready at twelve or he darts in at eleven-thirty with: "Can you fix me something, quick? I'm in a hurry." This is the same tune that most wives sing from California to Maine, living in penthouses and haciendas, tents or travel trailers.

My husband leaves his pajamas on the floor along with yesterday's levies, socks, and slippers. He refuses to answer the telephone when he is sitting right by it and I'm out in the kitchen with my hands in the dough. He leaves the top off the toothpaste, dries his hands on the guest towel, and turns the newspaper inside out, upside down, with part in the bathroom and the other sections — wherever they fall. When he takes a hand at cooking, which he likes to do, he can soil every pot and pan available.

The sight which confronts me after I returned home from an absence of about four days is typical. There are partially empty packages of bread and boxes of crackers scattered about the house. Frying pans, containing various amounts of grease, rest haphazardly on the sink and stove. Egg shells, milk cartons, grapefruit rinds mingle with empty cans, used dishes, and paper napkins. Newspapers, magazines, letters, and shirts litter the chairs and floor. The brush of Hurricane Edna's passage couldn't have wrought more havoc. No assortment of jigsaw puzzle pieces could have been as perplexing as this tangle of kitchen scramble.

Rather than being indignant with the disarray, I was amused. Intrigued with the challenge of restoring things to order, I thought of the kitchen as assuming the status of Exalted Supreme Center of Attention during my absence. Like Cinderella, everything was restored to order, not at midnight, but upon the return of the dragon mistress of the house.

A stockman makes no effort to stay clean while working in the out of doors but resigns himself to wearing worn and sturdy clothing. But dressed up in his "Saturday night goin' a steppin' togs" he is a pretty good looking fellow. His driver's license reads: Height — 6 feet; weight — 176 pounds; Hair — brown; Eyes — black. This description is accurate as far as it goes but it fails to mention the flecks of gray at his temples and the twinkle that hovers behind the piercing brightness of his eyes.

His smile, too, can be warm and comforting, but he doesn't always smile. He is, after all, just normal with a temper which flares sky-high like an exploding firecracker when things go wrong. His innate desire to do everything right and on schedule strikes a match to the temper fuse when complications prevent the execution of his immediate plan. He expresses his frustration in song.

The song he sings isn't musical but always has the same words. According to his vernacular there are an uncountable number of things in the world which are offsprings of a certain type of family pet. Fortunately they are all "sons." I quake in my boots as I live in fear of the day that the old bitch will have a daughter and I'll learn that I, too, have joined the clan.

During an unusually cold spell of weather a few years ago, the ice on the roads, fences, and trees was the central focus for the cowboy's wrath. Kerosene burners, sledge hammers, and axes were all used as methods of attacks on the frozen water troughs. By the time the water began gurgling up between the floating blocks of ice, the thirsty stock that had been standing there begging for a drink had all departed, frightened by the noise and profane activity.

The cowboy began to sing just after breakfast when the pickup, his main mode of transportation, wouldn't start. The song went something like: "this — of a — won't start; the — of a — stock are starving; the Mexicans will be sitting on their — of a — ???s. Go get me some boiling water if the — of a — pipes aren't frozen." Then, some time later, when the motor fired, he turned on me with: "What in the world are you standing out here in the — of a — cold for? Don't you have sense enough to stay inside where it is warm?" and with those kind and loving words, the cowboy and his song drove off to find the Mexicans and take feed to the livestock.

This is just another characteristic a hard working husband has in common with others. But "All work and no play makes Jack a dull boy," and Jack is anything but dull.

Most outdoorsmen are sportsmen at heart, and Jack is no exception. He thrills with exhilaration when an outlaw steer runs from the herd and a good horse gets after it. The poised movements of the pony as it pauses, weight on it's haunches, front feet almost off the ground, waiting for the steer's next move fills him with pride. He takes real joy as he sees an alert stock dog crouching with muscles taut as it stalks an errant sheep. He relaxes on

58

the banks of spring fed Cedar Creek waiting for the bobbing cork to disappear.

Football, deep sea fishing, rodeos, horse racing, and baseball all hold a special interest for my husband, but his main diversion is playing with the dogs. He takes them with him when he goes for a swim in the stock tank or makes a night run hunting fox or coons. He tests the accuracy of his shooting skill by popping off the clothespins on my line and, just to keep in practice, tosses a loop over the corner post, at a passing chicken, or even the family cat. The cat isn't the only thing he teases for he takes a fiendish delight in telling about my culinary expertise.

Butch, a boy from Junction who was helping us, came in for lunch before Jack and said he needed to get back to the pens as soon as possible. I had thawed some Red Snappers we caught on a trip to the Gulf and fried one for him. Later, when Jack came in, I prepared one in the same manner for him. One bite and my husband exploded. "Woman," he shouted, "you didn't take the scales off this fish."

And poor Butch had eaten everything on his plate.

CHAPTER 19

Night was slowly dying behind the hills when Jack crawled out of bed and, with drops of perspiration glistening on his brow, pulled on his boots.

"It is going to be a scorcher," he announced from where he stood looking out the window. "You should be getting up, shouldn't you? The sooner we get out there, the better."

He was right, as usual. The day was a scorcher. It was one of those sweltering days when the very air seemed heated by a furnace. Our eyes smarted, our ears burned, and the horses were lathered. Early as it was, the sultry morning air was unbearably close as we rode with shirt tails out, sleeves rolled up, and heads tucked.

Progress through the pasture was reduced to a snail's pace as the cattle, too, were affected by the heat. They did perk up and move more freely as we came out into the clearing around the pens. Some stopped at the salt lick; the others headed for the water troughs. Our shadows were directly beneath us when we loosened the girths on our saddle horses and headed for the house.

Listening to the noon weather broadcast, we heard the announcer say, "A blue Norther is due to cover the state, bringing with it much colder weather, plunging temperatures well below freezing."

Impossible we thought as we mounted our horses and started the cattle on the rest of their way to the south pasture.

The first indication of relief came from the animals, proving their sensitivity to climatic conditions. The cattle seemed to relax, to move more freely, our saddle horses lifted their heads to sniff the air and no longer needed urging.

The cowboy and I must have unconsciously felt the change but were surprised when the sun suddenly disappeared and an awesome darkness embraced the land. An ominous calm, as though the world was holding its breath, preceded the violent eruption of roaring wind. The very ground seemed to rock while trees quivered and dead brush swirled and danced before us. Boris had made his grand entry with all the pomp and ceremony nature could provide.

Shirt sleeves were pulled down, collars turned up, and heads averted to avoid the stinging blasts of cold. The cattle practically sailed before us and were soon turned loose in their new stomping ground. It was good and cold as we turned back into the wind.

"Jack," I said. "I'm so cold my hands are numb. I can't even feel the bridle reins."

"I know," he answered, "so are mine. There isn't anything between us and the North Pole but a barbed wire fence and it is at the other end of the pasture."

If only that deep dark blue cloud which twisted and whistled about us that day could be transferred to the silver screen, the director would make a fortune overnight. Nothing that the best of man can do will ever compare to the marvelous creations of nature.

Those of us living in her backyard are treated to the many spectacular artistic presentations her ever changing moods conjure up. The world is one large palate, and she, the greatest artist of all, produces her scenes of beauty or horror, peace or turmoil on a gigantic stage.

The appropriateness of her backdrops is controlled by the revolving seasons, moving from spring's green awakening to summer's warm browns, through autumn's brilliant reds and yellows to winter's glistening sparkles of white.

The rising and setting sun, twinkling stars, and flashing lightning provide effects of bright or dark illumination spotlighted by the moon. Objects and animals are the actors on this stage, each with a story to tell.

Windmills whine when the wind shifts direction; slamming gates announce someone's arrival or departure; the scream of a peacock signals alarm; hens cackle when an egg is laid; roosters

61

herald the coming of a new day. It is eating time when horses neigh or cows moo, and there is happiness when birds chirp, cats purr, or squirrels romp.

Weather, like a Supreme Court Judge presiding over a special session, influences the activities of our days and the cowboy has his method of predicting what the decision will be. If there is a double layer of clouds, he looks for rain. He thinks a high wind out of the east for several days is also a good sign of moisture. He even hits the bull's-eye occasionally on the strength of having slick sheared goats in the pasture and no one to shed them.

A rain in the morning, he says, is like an old woman's dance, it doesn't last very long.

Lewis, an old-timer from these parts, has a superstitious belief for every occasion. He speaks of the south wind as "that ole she-devil." When the land is fanned by the rough, harsh breath of wind from the south for days, he says: "That ole she-devil is going after a load of ice. You betta look out." And sure enough, in a few days she switches around to the north and comes flying by dumping her chilling cargo down our backs.

He considers it bad luck for the smoke from a campfire to follow a person about, and the hoot of an owl predicts misfortune. "You betta turn ober ya shoe," he warns if a dog howls in the night. "If yo don't, thars gonna be a death in yo family, fer sure."

The moon, according to tradition, has a great deal to do with climatic conditions. There are "dry" and "wet" moons, a circle around one foretells rain, and witches prowl when it is "full." "A rainbow at morning, sailors take warning; rainbow at night, sailors delight." The "signs" of the zodiac must be observed for they influence bleeding, growing, conceiving, and cutting hair.

Ranch people watch the behavior of the animals to indicate a change. Sheep and goats, which go into the wind at bedding time, can anticipate shifts in direction. Morning finds them in the north end of the pasture when the wind was out of the south at dark. Spooky horses, romping calves, and cackling hens also deserve consideration.

Thunder in February, moss on the north side of trees, and a heavy coat of hair or early flight of birds also have a special meaning. Most of the time we have a pretty good idea what to expect, but, like when the blue Norther took us by surprise, we just have to take what comes. Like it or not!

CHAPTER 20

A few hundred yards off to the right of one of the roads leading to our house is a sign nailed to a tree. It is just an old piece of cardboard upon which the words: "kep out by rder of Gawd" are rudely printed, but it serves its purpose. No one ever willingly disregards this notice.

The sign guards the entrance to the camp of an old man whose days, apparently, are spent in cutting cedar. That he cuts cedar we know, for the evidence is all around, but what else he does is speculation.

The man and his sign were there when Jack took over the ranch, and we don't know much more about him now than we did then.

There are those who suggest he might have been a World War II spy with his wireless equipment assured sanctuary by the forbidding sign. Others believe him to be crazy, a fugitive from the law, maybe just a draft dodger. Whatever he is, we know him to be a cantankerous old man with a definite penchant for privacy and silence.

The area protected by his sign is completely obscured by thick clumps of cedar and sits on a little knoll from which he has a good view of all the ranch roads.

Vast acres of the bushy, squat shrub covered the valleys and hillsides when we first saw the ranch. Now the evergreen's dark foliage serves as a complimentary backdrop, in the fall, for the bright yellow of the wild Chinaberry trees and the brilliant red of the Sumac and Spanish Oak. The cedar contributes to the picturesqueness of the country but that is about all it is good for.

Cedar is like a big octopus with tentacle spreading out in all directions obscuring the sunlight and preventing any other growth. The trees are so close together that man's progress through its domain is difficult if not impossible. Low hung branches interlocking their lacy fingers as barricades dare the rider to force an entrance. These brakes are further undesirable as they provide excellent hiding places for reluctant stock, breeding areas for fires, and seclusion for predatory animals.

Removing this undesirable coverage from the land was one of Jack's first prerogatives. Men wielding hand axes would go through the thickets, selecting and cutting the straight tree trunks for fence posts, the limbs and branches for stays. Then giant dozers began to crawl across the land, crushing and uprooting everything in their paths.

The old man of the sign, whom we called Mr. Pierson, worked alone as he hunted, chopped, and shaped the posts and stacked them in piles ready for market but, as he worked, his rifle was always close at hand.

I had been on the ranch for three years before catching a glimpse of him and then he stood looking at me from behind a tree. He seemed just a pitiful little ole man who looked more like a scarecrow or a frightened animal than someone to be feared.

A trucker, wanting to buy a load of his posts, was idly walking near the camp waiting for the chopper when he was confronted with the rifle in his face and Mr. Pierson's snarling eyes behind it, hissing something like: "I'se bin thar onst nd I ken go back. You jest git ute ov here, quick, nd neber kum back."

Another time the rifle was pointed at a traveler, who wanted to ask directions. From all indications Mr. Pierson would use his gun if provoked which we have no intention of doing. A rifle, brandished promiscuously by an irrational and disturbed old man whose sanity is questionable is sufficient reason for all of us to leave him to the privacy he desires.

Buster, who more than anyone else, goes out of his way to avoid the recluse, was paralyzed with fright the night he inadvertently found himself in the center of the forbidden area.

It happened one night we drove down to the beaver dam on Cedar Creek to see if the dogs would jump some coons. No sooner had we stopped the pickup than they were out and running.

"I don't like it," Jack said. "They're running too fast and straight. I'm afraid they are after a deer."

"But I thought you said they wouldn't chase deer," I commented.

"Old Soupy won't, but I don't know what the pups will do," replied the cowboy. "If it is a deer, I think he will come back." And, even as he spoke, the black and white spotted Walker hound trotted into sight, alone.

We could still hear the barking in the distance, so Buster and Shorty followed the dogs while Jack drove around, hoping to head the wild pups.

We had been waiting at the appointed meeting place for about ten minutes when the moon-washed silence was broken by a thrashing like a herd of stampeding buffaloes.

Eighteen-year-old Buster, breathing like a thrashing machine, staggered to us, too short of breath to speak. He looked as if he had been worked over by a bobcat or run through a meat grinder. His shirt was torn, blood oozed from long scratches on his face and hands. His jeans were snagged, and he walked with a decided limp. Most noticeably of all was the fact that his hat was missing.

"Where is your hat?" was the first thing Jack said. Shorty, coming up behind the boy, began to shake with laughter as he said, "He jes plum run out from under it."

"Yep, shore did," confirmed the lad, "and I shore ain't gonna go back after et."

We soon learned that the deer, with the barking and yapping dogs at its heels, had run directly into the old cedar chopper's camp. The sight of the old man standing there behind his trusty gun had frightened the wits out of the boy. Running blindly through the cut cedar branches strewn about on the ground, he had been tripped, clutched, and trapped in their clutches.

The next morning the dogs came home, sore-footed and drawn, but Buster had no sympathy for them.

Mr. Pierson is afraid of something we know. With the cunningness of a hunted animal he creeps about, standing immovable behind trees or rocks, crawling along the ground, and going about under cover of darkness. No one has ever seen him very far away from the general vicinity of his hillside and never without his gun.

Along with his peculiarities and eccentricities, this quaint old recluse has remained a mystery, living alone in a ramshackle lean-to covered with flattened out tin cans and discarded boards with a simple thatched roof. His sign is a warning everyone honors.

We leave him alone, allowing him to remain, because the posts he cuts are works of art in their uniformity. The many acres he has cut with his axe now look like a well-manicured lawn. The rank, dark thicket where predatory animals once lived and bred is now a haven for livestock grazing in the sunshine.

CHAPTER 21

We must have looked like ghostly forms as we rode along, each silently contemplating the expectations of the drive. Roundup time is always difficult. This time we would be looking for one hundred horses in a twenty-four hundred acre pasture and doing it the hard way. The easy way is to haunt the watering places but, in the Dillingham, water is everywhere. Cedar Creek, that beautiful little spring-fed stream I fell in love with on my first ride on the ranch, flows through the entire pasture and there are several windmills as well.

The crescendo of busy, bustling country noises created by the approaching dawn synchronized their sounds with the increasing light as we entered the horse pasture and began drifting further and further apart. Both Ox and Jack were on my left and the other four on my right. Our plan was to work our way to the back fence and bring the horses around to the right.

Working my way in and out of the thickets, always preceded by the ever-shortening shadow my horse and I cast before us, the idea of possible trouble had never entered my head. The going was slower than usual due to the heavy sogginess of the ground, and I thought nothing of reaching the fence before the others.

A cold chill gripped the young man's heart when he saw the red and white paint running toward the group of horses grazing in the opening. The sight of a riderless horse with reins flying and stirrups flapping in the breeze can mean but one thing. The rider was in trouble and must be found.

Time seemed to stand still for Ox as he followed the tracks left in the muddy ground by the running horse. The tracks led him through rough terrain where low, thorny agarita and scrub oak mingled together to form a veritable jungle. Cedar and cat-claw branches snatched at his face and clung to his legs. Passage became slower and more difficult when he reached the arroyo where the merging canyons cut deep ravines with their slippery sides and steep banks. Mired down with anxiety, the man was caught off guard when, wading along the edge of one of these gullies, his horse spooked at an object in the bottom. There, at the foot of a deep cut trail, he sighted my husband walking with downcast eyes as he followed the muddy tracks left by his fleeing mount.

Neither man said a word at first as Jack reached for the reins of the horse being led by Ox and mounted. Together, they turned back in the direction from which he had started. Ox to pick up the bunch he had left grazing and Jack to continue his search. Just before leaving, Jack put out his hand.

"Thanks," he said in a voice full of emotion. "I owe you, and I'll never forget."

Later, as we unsaddled our horses, one of the hands noticed the rancher walking with a limp and inquired:

"Hey, what happened to you, Boss?"

"Nothing much, just had a little trouble." He answered casually, trying to avoid an explanation, but we insisted upon hearing the story.

"Well, soon after we broke up, I found Paddy and his gang but they spied me and took off. I knew my horse wasn't fast enough to head them so I thought I'd take a shortcut through the canyon. Spanish slipped and nearly fell on the way down, and I bounced out of the saddle and lost the reins. I was able to grab the back of the saddle and strings but my spur hung behind the horn. The poor horse was struggling to gain his balance among the rocks and slippery bank, and I didn't help any. Sure thought I was a gonna, but, when we hit bottom and he started pitching, the spur came loose and I hit the ground. Ox can tell you the rest."

There is still a deep gash across the seat of the saddle made by his spur but the cuts and scratches have healed and the tattered shirt and jeans discarded. The cowboy had mounted his horse and gathered and penned the hundred head, which was what he had started out to do.

68

Our neighbor, Chester Stapp, was not so lucky when he hung to the horse he was riding one day.

I had just finished feeding the chickens that morning when I saw the approaching car and heard the incessant blowing of the horn.

"Quick," called the excited driver, "Check to see if the ambulance is on its way. A man has been badly hurt back there." He pointed in the direction from which he had come.

The ambulance passed me as I reached the gate so I followed as it wound its way toward the beckoning woman.

When I helped lift Chester on the stretcher, I had difficulty finding a place to put my hands. His back was badly mangled. Peggy crawled in beside her husband and the ambulance started on its way to the hospital. Chester died before reaching it.

Those of us left behind discussed the possibilities of how the accident had occurred. Most thought that the horse had sucked back when the rancher reached over to unlatch the gate. This probably threw the rider off balance and his foot, which was small for a man, slipped through the stirrup. What we did know was that the young horse had not stopped running and kicking until the boot came off and the man fell.

I learned later that the couple had started riding toward the road when the woman remembered she had left the fire burning under the beans. They planned where to meet across the road and she turned back toward the house. That meeting never took place.

Peggy and I became very close friends and did everything we could to help each other.

She drove into her garage late one night and saw a rattler coiled against the wall. She told us how she had rushed into the house for her gun and shot at the snake. She thought it was hit, but it slithered off and disappeared beneath her front porch.

"Connie," she said over the phone the next morning, "can you come down and hold the flashlight for me. I want to crawl under the house and look for a snake I think I wounded last night."

Jack and one of the Mexicans drove up just as I was leaving, and, when I told him where I was going, said, "Wait until I get a gun. Pedro and I will go with you."

The flashlight shone on the rattlesnake, coiled in the corner.

Pedro shot and killed it. He then pulled it out for us to see. As snakes so often do, it was still twitching and squirming, so Peggy held the muzzle of her single shot .22 to its head and released the trigger.

Click, was all we heard.

I cringe to think, even now, of that woman planning to go beneath her house armed with a gun loaded with one shell — a dud.

CHAPTER 22

The cowboy and his wife are living today in a rapidly changing world. Civilization, not content with knocking on our door, has forced it ajar and stands with one foot inside. Within the last six years we have witnessed the arrival of yellow-painted vehicles with the circled State Highway Construction on their sides. We have seen them swarm, like large ants, across the land following the rasping screech of the big cat's blades. We have heard the incessant roar and rumble of dynamite and the grinding of steam rollers. We have smelled the stink of tar. We have seen the detour signs come down and watched the ebb and flow of passing travel wash along the winding ribbon of progress.

Having adjusted ourselves to this encroachment upon our privacy, we relax and sit on our front porch observing the never ending roll down the highway. We see long, expensive sedans with out-of-state licenses, loaded with straw sombreros, bottles of agua caliente, and embroidered mantillas from Mexico. We see trucks, with their human cargo sandwiched like sardines, carrying migrant workers to Northern Kansas. The tranquility of the night is disturbed by bawling cattle as they are hauled to the stockyards or slaughter pens. Refrigerated trucks bringing fruit and vegetables from the valley meet others heavy with cotton or cedar posts.

Like sitting at the bedside of a dear friend, we feel the pulse of the road and count the beats of humanity's struggle to survive.

Each day the Old West slips further away, while the new gains strength and promise.

With these changing times, trips to town are no longer limited to once a week and can be made as easily as running down to the corner store. The women are participating in church and community activities, study clubs, literary societies, and attending socials and musicals. The men are taking time to go to church, International Club luncheons, and to see the latest movies at the drive-in. Neighbors drop in for supper and stay for a game of Canasta or to see the fights on TV.

Simple is the life the cowboy has built for himself. It is constructed on a foundation of clean living, of pure contentment, and it is substantiated by hard work and satisfaction. He has earned the right to "sit by the side of the road and watch the rest of the world go by."

1992 ADDITION

The cowboy's days of sitting "by the side of the road" ended in 1980. God called him to the range of eternity, where the animals were in need of someone to restore the gloss to their hides and put flesh on their bodies.

Let there be no moaning at the bar when the gate is shut on me. My cowboy husband will be waiting here, sitting tall in the saddle on old Paddy and holding Danger Boy's bridle reins. Together we will ride the beautiful pastures and climb the rugged hills. Maybe we'll find little Johnny Mendoza's bud in the Heavenly Garden and smell the fragrance of the flower. "The joys we share as we linger there, none other can compare."

Afterword

By Gail Woerner

People like Constance Douglas Reeves are few and far between. When one is fortunate enough to become acquainted with such a person, one's life is enriched tenfold because her spirit, vigor, and razor-sharp wit is very infectious.

A former student of Connie's, Jack Long of San Antonio, who is also a friend of mine, took me to Kerrville to meet her. At seventy-six years of age, Jack enjoys retirement by visiting with rodeo greats of yesteryear and friends who have spent their life involved with and promoting the West. As an author bent on recording rodeo history before it is lost, I occasionally pen articles for magazines interested in western phenomena. Jack just knew I had to meet Connie Reeves.

We went to her well-kept home located on a quiet street in Kerrville. As she greeted us at the front door, she informed us our timing was perfect. She had just finished *mowing* her lawn and *repairing* her television set. Although Connie does not see well enough to drive, read, or watch TV, one would not realize she had a sight problem or that she was ninety-two years old as she moved around her home with enthusiasm and precision.

The cozy living room was filled with western memorabilia. A large 1950s vintage photograph on the wall of her husband, Jack Reeves, and several other cowboys, taking a few minutes in the shade of a covered porch during a searing-hot Texas summer day. Other paintings of horses told us what was dear to Connie.

It only took a short time to feel I had known Connie all my

life. Not only did I like her instantly, I also knew she would become a special friend. She spoke openly about a variety of subjects, and although she had a forty-year jump on me, we shared many feelings toward family, horses, and the West.

During lunch at a local Mexican food restaurant, this charming nonagenarian greeted various employees as old friends. Time passed much too quickly and before I realized it, it was time to go. I knew I had found someone who would make a difference in my life.

Camp Waldemar holds a Women's Week in late September, which I attended in 1994. Women from across the country spend a week at the camp enjoying a variety of activities, including horseback riding, golf, tennis, archery, and canoeing on the Guadalupe River. The women can also choose a series of craft lessons or seminars on subjects from microwave cooking to photography. Others fill the week with massages, manicures, facials, and lectures – generally escaping the problems women face daily.

Many of the women were former campers coming back to the site where fond memories of their first experiences at camp as young girls were created. The attendees were comprised of professional women from a variety of fields, mothers and housewives, of all ages.

The first morning of camp I signed up to go on a breakfast trail ride. I was excited to see my new friend, Connie, and have an opportunity to ride horses with her.

It was a perfect September morning in the Texas Hill Country. The grass glittered with drops of dew while the last remains of morning fog lifted from the Guadalupe River. A mockingbird hidden in a nearby live oak announced the new day. Connie was busy at work in the stables, preparing the horses for the ride. At ninety-two years of age (as of this printing), Connie had followed this morning ritual for fifty-eight years. The white-haired cowgirl, dressed in form-fitting jeans, instructed half a dozen assistants, as she decided which horses would require English saddles and which would don western saddles. After fifty-eight camp seasons, the routine was quite familiar, as was the six-hours-a-day in the saddle Connie spent performing her responsibilities. Her assistants were women who had learned their horsemanship from her – some as young campers at Waldemar.

With the summer camp season at a close, owner, Marsha

Elmore, sees that Camp Waldemar is utilized year-round. Corporations use the facilities for seminars, church groups hold retreats, and there are special weekends for families or mother-daughter get-togethers. Recently Waldemar has opened a Bed & Breakfast venue offering cozy rooms uniquely decorated and designed with one-of-a-kind classic cowboy decor.

As we prepared for our ride that September morning, twenty-two women waited for Connie to match rider to mount. She based her selections on the rider's ability and her thorough knowledge of each horse's nature and attitude. After mounting a gleaming bay Arabian gelding named Macho, Connie made sure each rider was comfortable, that each had their stirrups the proper length, and that everyone was happy. There were no complaints — the weather was perfect, the setting one of the most magnificent the Hill Country has to offer, and the camaraderie between the women was beginning to develop.

We had not trailed far before it was evident that every rider had a special admiration for this *doyenne de equestriennes*. She had achieved what we all were looking for — longevity, health, and spirit!

Following Connie's lead, the assistants moved back and forth on horseback between the riders, to make sure everyone was at ease and had no problems. As we rode single-file following the trail up the side of a hill through a heavily wooded stand of cedar, riders conversed with other riders in front or in back of them. Suddenly, the horse in front of Connie started to buck. Although her eyesight is dim, Connie knew there was a problem and immediately moved her mount forward to help the rider. Before Connie could do a thing, Macho began to buck frantically. A nest of ground hornets had been disturbed, and they were attacking the horses. Connie was tossed to the ground, and she LANDED ON TOP OF THE NEST. The hornets started attacking Connie immediately! Riders jumped from their horses and covered Connie with jackets, or whatever was available, to keep the stinging hornets from her. A doctor and a nurse on the ride quickly afforded her medical assistance. Others calmed the frightened horses, and as quickly as the incident had occurred, it was over.

Connie sustained three broken ribs, a partially collapsed lung, a broken wrist, plus too many hornet stings to count. She was quickly transported to a San Antonio hospital, where she was treated and placed in intensive care until the doctors were certain she would be all right.

Back at Waldemar, campers prayed, concentrating on their love and hope for her recovery. Upon her release from the hospital, a short nine days later, she returned to her home in Kerrville to recuperate.

By late October, a month after the accident, the lively lady of ninety-three years, went on a trail ride in Arizona. Although she and another friend enjoyed the event in a four-wheel-drive vehicle, instead of horseback, her tenacity and determination to keep from being sidelined was admirable.

The accident occurred during Connie's work responsibilities, so Camp Waldemar filed the proper papers for Texas Worker Compensation Insurance. The State office called the camp after receiving the forms and said someone must have made a mistake. When Julie, in the camp office, inquired as to the mistake, they said, "You listed the claimant's birth date as 1901."

"That is correct," confirmed Julie.

The insurance company, Texas Workers' Compensation Insurance Fund, has verified that Connie Reeves is the oldest claimant they have ever paid! In fact, prior to this claim, the oldest claimant had been eighty-two years of age, according to Steve Sadler, Director of Special Projects, for the company. Mr. Sadler and crew of video cameramen returned to the camp to film a reenactment of the accident (without the hornet stings).

Constance Douglas was indeed born in 1901 and raised in Eagle Pass, Texas, on the Texas-Mexican border. Her father, William Constant Douglas, was a District Judge for an area of Texas that reached as far west as Alpine and Marfa. Her mother, Ada, was the daughter of Alfred Wallace and Esther Kincaid Wallace. Grandfather Wallace was raised on a ranch near Marathon, while Grandmother Wallace was raised on the Kincaid ranch near Uvalde. Constance was an only child.

Her paternal grandfather, Douglas Ross, came to the United States from England. He was born into English nobility, but because he was the youngest child, he felt that there was no future for him in England. Douglas eventually dropped the Ross name. He became a member of the Texas militia assigned to the Eagle Pass area, where he met fifteen-year-old Lula Terry, and they married. William Constant Douglas was born of this union.

76

Connie's maternal grandfather always made sure she had a horse to ride. Spending many hours with him riding gave her the opportunity to absorb much of his knowledge of horses, thus learning how to deal with the four-footed friends. She also credits him with much of the "horse sense" she acquired about things other than equine.

When Connie was sixteen years old, the family moved to San Antonio. Mr. Douglas continued his law practice and Connie decided she wanted to follow in his footsteps as an attorney. After attending Texas Women's University, then known as College of Industrial Arts (The State College For Women), and receiving her Bachelor of Science degree, she went on to the University of Texas at Austin. As she worked toward a law degree, she was active on campus in a variety of ways including acting and participating in the Curtain Club, the drama organization. Other activities included being elected Chairman of the Women's Council, the legislative branch of student government (She was the first woman assembly member from the school of law at the university.); vice-president of the school of law; and in extemporaneous speaker winning second place with her speech titled "Social Influence of the Movies."

During Connie's years at the University of Texas, it was a goal of the school and its students to build a home for Texas "spirit," which in 1924 led to a major fund-raising campaign. Connie held the responsible position of Vice-Chairman of the Central Student Committee. Her co-leader was Cecil Chamberlain. Their efforts resulted in the building of Memorial Stadium.

Upon leaving law school, lacking only the bar exam, Connie returned to San Antonio and took a teaching position at Main Avenue High School for the 1925 academic year. The economic pressures of the Depression were affecting the economy, and no jobs were available for junior lawyers. While teaching English and speech, Connie also started the first pep squad in San Antonio in 1928.

In 1932 a new high school, Thomas Jefferson, was opened and Connie went there to teach physical education. By October of that year, she had formed a second pep squad to cheer for the new school's football team. It was a novel squad, named the Lassos, and wore western-styled uniforms consisting of blue flannel skirts, a blue bolero jacket, red satin blouse, a pearl gray Stetson hat, and a lasso rope attached by a loop at the waist of their skirt.

Johnny Reagan, a trick rope artist from England, who taught campers to trick rope during the summer camp season at Camp Waldemar, introduced the squad to twirling a short rope. The lasso operated on a swivel and a slight wrist action would put the rope in motion and was simple to use. One hundred and twenty girls, all twirling lassos in unison was a thrilling sight to behold, and it wasn't long before they were performing as a service organization at practically all state and national conventions held in San Antonio, as well as major athletic events.

After graduating from Thomas Jefferson High School, Jack Long, a trick roper, would assist Connie and teach a selected group of eighteen to twenty students all sorts of rope tricks. Once they learned the simpler tricks such as a flat loop, stepping in and out and to skip the spoke, he taught them to perform with longer ropes. They learned the famous Texas Sip and the Wedding Ring.

By 1939 the Lassos' reputation had spread nationwide. They performed on a Goodwill and Educational Tour which traveled to New York for the World's Fair, to Washington, D.C., Philadelphia, Chicago, and Niagara Falls. In the early 1940s Hollywood came and filmed a movie with Jane Withers, a young actress of the day portraying the part of a Lasso pep squad member.

Times were not easy, the Depression took its toll, and Connie's teaching salary was her family's primary source of income. In addition to her teaching responsibilities, Connie and Harry Hamilton, a teacher, coach, and her fiancé, had a riding stable on the Hamilton family's one hundred acres at the edge of San Antonio. His coaching responsibilities kept him at football or basketball practice most days after school. Connie took the responsibility of working with the horses, and she also taught horseback riding.

Although she had been raised riding western style, the delightfully curious horsewoman found a new interest in riding and teaching English style. On one occasion Connie spotted her mother's car approaching the stables. She was certain Grandfather Wallace would be in the car as well, and as she was in the middle of an English riding lesson, she immediately quit posting and tried to sit as if she were riding western. Ringing in her ears was the memory of her grandfather's voice saying, "Don't let me ever see you bobbing up and down like a 'Bolly Englishman'." Her great respect for her grandfather and his approval overshadowed anything else she would do. This granddaughter would never lose the respect and love for this man who taught her so many wonderful lessons as she grew into adulthood.

Some of the stable horses were owned by Hamilton and some were Connie's. She showed horses owned by both of them, often bringing home ribbons. Her horsemanship and knowledge of horses became well known and she was often asked to judge horse shows in the area. Little did she realize how much of her life would revolve around her friends of the four-footed variety.

Not all of Connie's time was limited to the horse-set. She served as president of the San Antonio Girl Scout Leaders Association. She also spent some summers in Kawaji Camp in Minnesota, teaching drama and horseback riding.

Camp Waldemar became a reality in 1926 under the direction of Ora Johnson. Miss Johnson was an outstanding educator in the San Antonio area and always had a dream to develop a camp for young ladies to help them grow into "finer, nobler women as a result of the lofty ideals and standards made desirable at the camp."

Miss Johnson came from a family very active in the world around them. Her grandfather, Joshua Foster Johnson, was one of seven Texas legislators who joined Sam Houston in voting against secession in 1861. Her father was a Baptist minister and instrumental in moving Baylor University from Independence to Waco, Texas. Miss Johnson had four brothers and two sisters, and all remained close. One of her brothers Col. W. T. Johnson, in addition to accumulating a large number of ranch holdings, became the premier rodeo producer of the 1930s. At various times during the off-season, the rodeo horses were kept at the camp and the camp employed many rodeo hands, when the colonel did not need their services. In fact Johnny Reagan, the aforementioned trick roper, traveled and performed at Johnson's rodeos.

Miss Ora Johnson had high expectations for Camp Waldemar. She was a firm leader, demanded a great deal from her staff and counselors, and felt the responsibility to build the character of these young, innocent ladies very strongly. Miss Ora died in 1931, and her niece, Doris Johnson, who is the daughter of brother, Joshua Foster Johnson, took over the direction of the camp. She continued to follow Miss Ora's ideals.

Connie Douglas came to Camp Waldemar in 1936 as a counselor of horseback riding. Campers were taught both English and Western riding. Jack Reeves, a cowboy and former competitor in Colonel Johnson's rodeos as well as other rodeos, was in charge of maintaining the camp horses. Connie and Jack communicated often about the horses and she found him wholesome, refreshing, and down-to-earth.

Prior to meeting Jack, Connie had broken her long engagement and ten-year association with Harry Hamilton. Living in San Antonio, many of Connie's suitors were military cadets and service personnel. She discovered that during peaceful times those in the military are prone to boredom and have a tendency to try to find some excitement. Some tried "getting out of line" but Connie did not appreciate their actions. She found her country-rodeo working associate, Jack, a most pleasant change. As their friendship and business association developed, they found they had much in common regarding their mutual interest in horses and the outdoors. In 1942 they tied the knot.

One fall, after the camp season was over, Jack took Connie to the famous Madison Square Garden Rodeo, where he had competed earlier. Connie has vivid memories of their trip and the curiosity of the New Yorkers toward her husband, dressed in his red-topped cowboy boots, and big western hat. "Like all cowboys, Jack didn't like to walk, and we had just finished doing some sight-seeing which required a bit of walking," recalled Connie. "Jack stopped to set a spell on a front step on the sidewalk. As the local people walked by, they made a big detour around his legs and watched him with curiosity. Finally a policeman sauntered by, twirling his billy club, as he looked at us suspiciously. Jack was certainly a novelty back there."

Jan Cannon, who has known Connie for forty-eight years, began this association as a camper. Jan relates that she was one of those campers that learned the do's and don't's from Connie very explicitly. "I was always in great trouble with her," Jan remembered. "If Connie said to go around a fallen log, on my horse, I would go over it. Fortunately for me, Connie recognized that I had spirit and appreciated my zest."

Jan remembered that Connie had nicknames for her campers. "I was Cannonball," she recalled, "and she knew every camper by name. She was respected and had a great sense of humor." Jan has been a counselor at Waldemar for forty-five years. She said when she first went to Waldemar she packed bathing suits and shorts as she was expecting to be counseling water activities. Unknown to Jan, Connie had picked her to be a part of her staff of horseback instructors. "I had to go to town and buy some jeans," laughed Jan. She learned so much from Connie and Jack during her years counseling with them.

Jan said that in the recent years she has completely forgotten their age differences. She also lives in Kerrville when not counseling at camp, and she remains a close friend to Connie, as well as a confidant, chauffeur, and on occasion reads to her.

"When I was teaching school in Lubbock and coaching the school tennis team," Jan recalled, "the team went by the Junction ranch on our way to a San Antonio tournament. I suggested we stop and see my friends, Connie and Jack. Little did I know they were in the process of castrating goats. My city-raised tennis team, dressed in Bermuda shorts and tennis shoes, watched this unfamiliar exercise with some awe and amazement. When their chore was completed, Connie fixed all of us a big meal and bid us farewell and good luck." Jan laughed and said, "Every time we went on an out-of-town tennis trip the team always wanted to go by the Reeves' ranch." Connie has always been an instant magnet to young people.

Aside from her man ranch chores, during their years at Junction, Connie participated in numerous community activities. Evolving from a men's nonsectarian Bible class in Junction in 1951, came a presentation involving half of the Junction community in a twelve scene recreation in pantomime of the story of Easter. Although the people of Junction preferred to remain anonymous, thousands of people came in carloads to witness this impressive annual event. Connie Reeves directed the pageant for seventeen years. In 1959 she was mistress of ceremonies at the Miss Mohair of the Universe Contest, held in Kerrville. Throughout the years, Connie has also given book reviews in the area.

When Jack became ill, Connie took the news as well as she could. His illness was grave and required relocating closer to medical facilities. They moved from the ranch at Junction to Kerrville. Although her responsibilities continued, Connie was at his side as much as she could. Jack died in 1985.

In 1979 Doris Johnson sold Camp Waldemar to Marsha

Elmore. By this time Miss Johnson was in failing health and realized she needed to pick her replacement with care and scrutiny if the camp were to continue on a similar path Marsha Elmore, former camper and counselor, was her choice.

Under direction of Marsha Elmore, and her family, the camp today not only has the high standards set by Miss Ora in 1926, but has evolved into a place of equally high standards for corporations, church groups, and private organization, during the off-season.

Connie is proud of her fifty-eight years at Waldemar. Not one camper has ever experienced a serious horseback riding accident. She attributes this to the fact that the camp owns their own horses and keeps them from year to year, allowing Connie and her staff to know the potential of each horse. The paperwork involved in keeping records of this program is lengthy and involves a great deal of time, but it is necessary. A horseback riding operation as successful as Camp Waldemar proves it. Liz Pipkin Pohl understudied Connie to take the reins of the horseback riding program at camp. However, according to Marsha Elmore, Connie will continue to consult with and advise the program director as long as she wants.

Camp Waldemar is extremely proud of their long-time association with Connie Douglas Reeves. The camp members are only the first in the long line of admirers of this grand lady. In fact, Marsha Elmore, a talented sculptress, is in the process of working on a life-size bronze of Connie and a horse, which will be placed in a prominent place on the grounds of the camp, near the entrance. What a tribute!

Connie has experienced a great deal in life—not because she has lived for ninety-three years, but because of her spirit. She does not hesitate to get involved, wherever she is, and she expects as much, if not more, from herself, as she expects from everyone else.

Connie has had several injuries, as a result of her time spent with horses. A horse's kick shattered her leg, which, after the pins were placed in her legs, required a lot of therapy. The pins did not work properly and one leg was shorter than the other. But she does *not* limp. She is strong-willed and refuses to let such incidents sideline her activities. Built-up boots have worked nicely, and if she is ever inconvenienced by pain, no one is aware.

Although she is knowledgeable and careful, someone as active as she, will take a "hit" now and then.

Although Connie's mother was a genteel lady who never went to the grocery store without hat and gloves, Connie feels that, in spite of the fact she spent most of her life quite differently, she took after her mother. Her mother had ridden sidesaddle as a girl and was a good marksman. Connie said her mother was disappointed in her because she was not as social as her mother expected her to be, nor did she enjoy getting together with the girls and playing bridge. Just imagine if Mrs. Douglas were here today watching her daughter excelling in any social setting, how extremely proud she would be.

Connie defines her vocabulary as "adolescent." Using the vernacular with which young people can relate she immediately is accepted by her young student-campers as a "with it" kind of gal. And she truly is! She is much more at home with young people she admits, but actually she has no problems with any age group.

Connie grew up at a time that she considered safe, she explains. "There was no fear then. We had no key to our home. We weren't afraid of cars or horses. Now, my grandmother's era was different. She was chased by Indians and that generation did know fear. My generation grew up with confidence," she concluded.

Connie did admit to having a concern about flying in large airplanes. But she quickly followed up with, "However, riding in a helicopter is a lark!"

The television media has found Connie a subject of much interest and she has been featured on John Pronk's "Texas Tales" and Bob Phillips "Hill Country Reporter," both programs about Texas phenomena. Connie is also asked to ride in numerous parades in Central Texas as a special Hill Country dignitary. Recently she has been asked to participate in Retama Race Track opening activities in San Antonio.

Connie Douglas Reeves is an inspiration to more people than we shall ever know — from her university days, through her teaching years in San Antonio and fifty-eight seasons at Camp Waldemar. She has influenced four generations, at least. Connie exemplifies three important aspects everyone strives to attain: a long life, a positive attitude, and the ability to adapt to an ever-changing world. A 90's kind of cowgirl — in more ways than one!

Connie and her mother, who also was a good rider – side saddle, that is.

Grandfather Wallace bought me my first horse at age five.

Connie ready for her horse show days in San Antonio.

Connie and Schoolboy clear a four foot jump at Waldemar.

Jack and Snort – a hard working pair.

Top left: Connie and Mr. George – a camp Palomino show horse.
Top right: Connie's children – she always had one or more.
Bottom: Riding the range together.

Jack during the Dude Ranch days.

Wondering if it's going to rain.

Top: Strange company – a border collie named "Trouble" and a fawn named "Mermaid."
Bottom: Jack and his round-up buddy, "Trouble."

Sheep round-up.

Connie greeting new campers as they get off the chartered buses.

Bus carnival, Connie style. . .

Top: Overnight with the "Hat's On" Club – Senior riders who do fun trips on horseback during the "off" season.
Middle: Waldemar riding department – includes teachers, wranglers, and groomers.
Bottom: Round-up time – the hunt is on for finding seventy plus head of horses in a 1,000 acre pasture where they have been wintered.

Waldemar Quadrille – a square dance on horseback ridden by twelve advanced riders.

"Ladies in the lead . . . And gents behind . . . All line up
For the circle grands . . ." '94 Waldemar Quadrille

Waterfront at Waldemar

Guardian swans at Waldemar

Acrobatics on horseback – monkey drill at Waldemar.

Field day competition in all sports – this is jousting.

Printed in the USA
CPSIA information can be obtained
at www.ICGtesting.com
LVHW012013300124
770046LV00011B/287